The Architectural Requirements
of
Protestant Worship

Humber Valley United Church showing narthex at left

The Architectural Requirements

of

Protestant Worship

VICTOR FIDDES

THE RYERSON PRESS—TORONTO

Published 1961

To
Norma

PRINTED AND BOUND IN CANADA BY THE RYERSON PRESS, TORONTO

CONTENTS

ILLUSTRATIONS

1

The Nature
of the Challenge

A study of the architectural requirements of Protestant worship is of
importance at any time, but particularly at a time of national growth and
economic prosperity such as Canada and the United States are now
experiencing. An explosive urban growth, the result of the rapid indus-
trialization of the past fifty years, is the most characteristic feature of the
physical changes that are taking place in the western world today. Authori-
ties on trends state that by the year 1980 Canada's population will have
almost doubled, with most of the growth concentrated in the already
burgeoning urban areas.

To the churches this growth means a tremendous challenge to provide adequate facilities for Christian worship and fellowship. The denomination with which the writer is most familiar, The United Church
of Canada, reports that in the twelve-year period from 1947 to 1958 three
hundred and sixty-one church units were erected in new extension areas
alone, a figure that represents almost fourteen per cent of all the pastoral
charges of the denomination. Other denominations could no doubt provide equally impressive figures in relation to their strength. All of them
agree that the demands will be great for many years to come. In the
United States church building has become almost a billion-dollar-a-year
industry, with no indication of any tapering of demand. Obviously the
time is opportune for the churches to provide themselves with good architecture for the future.

Particularly significant is the fact that this period of economic growth, with its resulting demand for greatly increased church facilities, coincides with a period of creativity in architecture and the allied arts. There have been other times of spectacular growth when churches were challenged to build, but at no time in the history of the North American peoples has architecture been stimulated as it is today. The present is both an experimental and a creative period for church design. Having long since broken from imitative styles, architecture has adapted itself both structurally and artistically to the possibilities that new materials and new techniques in construction provide. In this situation the design of a church presents an unusual challenge to the architectural profession, that of combining techniques and imagination in such a way that the design assumes a spiritual quality as an essential aspect of its practical function. It is the successful combination of these elements that means everything to good design in a church building.

Having been in creative periods of the past the patron of the best that architecture and the allied arts have had to offer, the Christian Church must not lose its opportunity in the new situation that confronts it in the twentieth century. Architecture today is eager to serve the Church; the ablest members of the profession are anxious for church assignments. This eagerness is not because of any economic benefit that accrues directly. Architects claim that they frequently lose money on churches — some of them claim that they actually find church building committees a little difficult to deal with! — but they like and want such work because they feel that ecclesiastical design challenges their skill. Contemporary architecture, we are told, is moving away from the sterile mechanical forms which, until recently, characterized the "continental style." Architecture is again claiming artistic inspiration for its new organic compositions. The church field, accordingly, presents attractive and tempting scope for experiment. The architect who in recent years has had more than his fill of engineering can at last get out from under the restrictions of the kind of design whose function has been determined almost solely by utilitarian ends. He can again become a creative artist.

It is precisely here, as we shall see, that the danger lies. The impulse of the artist to be creative carries with it a subtle danger to religion. The architect is tempted to substitute for the truth of revealed religion his own artistic insights. Recognition of this danger, however, should not blind the Church to the magnitude of the opportunity that confronts her in a creative period of architecture. Any failure to utilize the best that the architectural profession now has to offer can have only tragic consequences for the Church. The solution to the artistic problem is not to restrict the artist but to give him intelligent terms of reference.

There is no professional or practical difficulty for the architect in meeting the usual needs of the congregation as far as space and rooms are concerned, and most building committees, after careful study of the congregation's life and work, are able to offer the architect a fairly clear picture of their such physical requirements. Where most building committees fall down is in their failure to state clearly the logic of the building that they want to erect and the significance of the worship that takes place in it. The relationship between worship and other activities has not been carefully scrutinized; the theological principles which the building is designed to express, both in the worship and in the social and educational activities, have not been carefully set forth, perhaps not even considered. And yet precisely this is the knowledge which the architect most urgently needs. Since he is not himself a theologian and was never meant to be one, he has the right to expect a theological or ecclesiological frame of reference within which to do his best creative work.

Recognition of this fact is found in a statement of the 1957 Annual Report of the Department of Church Building to the Division of Home Missions of the National Council of Churches of Christ in the U.S.A. "For the future," states the report, "the major emphasis of the department should be on ideas rather than random activity. Much thought needs to be stimulated on the relationship of theology and church architecture and the educational philosophy underlying Christian education. There is also need for much research. Some of this should be sociological. . . . Some of it should deal with the practical problems of building."[1]

---

[1] 1958 Year Book, Division of Home Missions, National Council of Churches, p. 17.

The problem, understandably, is most serious within Protestantism and particularly within those churches that stand in the free and non-liturgical traditions so-called. In Roman Catholicism and in Orthodoxy the liturgical function of the building and the requirements of the sanctuary have been set forth in rubrics with which the architect can and must familiarize himself. We are told that before an architect undertakes an assignment for a Roman Catholic congregation he is called to the presbytery where he is made acquainted with the specific requirements of the liturgy in so far as they affect the design and fabric of the building. He is told where the altar must stand in relation to the parts of the sanctuary, where the priest must officiate and where the choir must not go. In many branches of Protestantism, however, no such direction is given. Requirements vary widely according to the customs and practices of denominations and even of local churches within the same denomination. Architects are so conscious of this diversity that they tend to overlook the unity that underlies the varied forms of worship and to treat the requirements of Protestantism as merely a matter of the congregation's individual choice.

The problem is admirably illustrated by the treatment given to Protestant churches in Thiry, Bennett and Kamphoefner's magnificent *Churches and Temples*—a book that has become something of a text for church builders in America today. The authors, after enunciating with painstaking care the liturgical requirements of the "Catholic" (sic!) church, dismiss Protestantism with the statement that "since Protestantism in America has no unity of faith and no architectural expression, it cannot really be treated as a single church." The editor concedes that since ninety per cent of the Protestant church members can be counted within twenty denominations it is possible to cover the architectural problem and solutions "by discussing the architecture of the largest denominations." The discussion proceeds, however, on no historical or theological ground, and it is hardly gratifying to the Protestant reader to find himself defined as "any Christian who denies the authority of the pope in Rome."

If this view that Protestant architecture is simply a matter of parochial choice is generally held by the profession one can appreciate the apprehension of architects who find themselves confronted with Protestant assignments, and one can understand how in the absence of theological direction they have come to rely upon purely aesthetic devices for the creation of a "worshipful" setting. In recent years this worshipful setting has been secured in one of two ways — either through the copying of archaic forms which have a sentimental appeal but are now redundant both architecturally and theologically, or through uncritical innovations and fads in so-called modern design where a striving for effect appears to be the most characteristic feature of the work. Both are dishonest solutions of the Protestant problem. The recovery of good architecture for Protestantism is not to be found in copying something that the Anglicans and the Lutherans took from Pugin and Ruskin in a nostalgic throwback to the middle ages. Nor is it to be found in some creative brain-wave of an individual who assumes that because a form has meaning for him it will have significance for a congregation that is supposed to be possessed of a sense of historic consciousness.

The recovery of good architecture for Protestantism is not primarily an architectural problem at all. First of all it is a theological problem. The church must know its function in the community and it must be able to tell its servants, the architects and the artists, precisely what they are supposed to achieve in a building devoted to the public worship of God, and then, may we add, *give them a free hand* in the execution of the design. Lacking such direction architects cannot be blamed for focusing their attention largely upon the aesthetic and artistic qualities of the buildings which they have been commissioned to design. For this unhappy state of affairs the Protestant churches themselves must accept the major responsibility.

Obviously the time has come for some deep soul-searching on the part of those who give leadership in the matter of Protestant church design. It is of paramount concern that those who provide the frame of reference within which the architects are to work should themselves be able to communicate clearly the basic needs of Protestant worship.

It is my conviction that the requirements of Protestant church architecture can best be met in terms of correspondence to historical requirements of worship which, for the most part, remain valid for all the denominations within the reformed tradition. The securing of good architecture for any one congregation accordingly involves the acceptance of principles that transcend its own needs and wishes. I believe that in the end of the day a building committee is likely to get more practical help from a long and informed view of church history than from a fevered pooling of local ideas and fancies. It is to the credit of the profession that the majority of architects recognize this fact and refuse to accommodate themselves to the passing whims of local building committees, the majority of which, I regret to say, appear to be liturgically uninformed and theologically illiterate.

The basic requirement of Protestant church architecture is that of a shared ministry of word and sacrament which is carried on in an environment of spiritual intimacy. The measure to which the ministry is shared and the degree of intimacy in which it is conducted may and do vary widely among the denominations and even among congregations in the same denomination, but the requirement itself remains basic. Analyze this need and it proves to be the constant factor in worship — alike in the experience of the early Christian Church and in the congregations that stand in the reformed tradition of Protestantism. Indeed it is basically ecumenical, affecting not only the various denominations within Protestantism but, to a certain extent, the whole Christian Church — Catholic, Protestant and Orthodox.

Even laymen who are quite uninformed in matters of church history and Christian liturgy are sensing that something of very great interest and importance is happening today in church architecture. It is not without significance that at the very time when the Protestant churches have become more liturgically minded the Roman Catholic Church has come to emphasize increasingly the unity of priest and people in the action of the Catholic liturgy. This trend should not be overemphasized — it would be a great mistake to assume that Protestantism and Roman Catholicism are about to meet at some midway point in liturgy and architecture — but it illustrates the fact that the unity that the divided bodies of Christendom do possess is revealing itself at that point where worship practices correspond to historical reality. This is precisely what we might expect, for if an ecumenical spirit exists at all it should manifest itself at that point where people actually do their worshipping. While, therefore, our concern in these pages is primarily with the architectural requirements of the various Protestant churches, and more particularly with the churches that stand in the reformed tradition, I should like to think that what follows will be of interest to students of church architecture in general.

2
Basic Concepts

I have defined the architectural requirements of Protestant worship rather loosely as the provision of a shared ministry of word and sacrament in an environment of spiritual intimacy. Christian worship expresses the action of the living risen Christ in the midst of his people, his giving himself to them in word and sacrament and the believers' renewal in him through the fellowship of the Church which is his body. I suggest that this definition corresponds to basic historical requirements of worship that can be traced back to the earliest days of the Church's life, and I would emphasize that it is at this "depth level" of "being in Christ" rather than in any organizational or institutional concept that the true nature of the Church's catholicity and unity is to be found. Before going on with our study of the fabric of the church building, therefore, let us take a closer look at Christian worship as it emerges in the New Testament picture and in the experience of the early Christian community.

The concept of the Church as the body of Christ precedes any formal organization of the institution, and emerges in the New Testament as the picture of an esoteric fellowship of believers — a body called, among other things, a *koinonia*. (This Greek word means literally "being associated with," or "becoming a sharer," and it is as adequate a single-word definition of the primitive church as can be found.) The apostle Paul writes of "the church which is his body, the fulness of him that filleth all in all"

(Ephesians 1:22,23). According to this New Testament picture the existence of the true church depends upon its being a community of persons functioning purposefully together because all its members are rooted in and branched from Jesus Christ its living head. The relationship of the persons, while intensely intimate and human, is based upon the experience of the worshipper's "being in Christ." "Where two or three are gathered together in my name, there am I in the midst of them" (Matthew 18:20). The Church exists only at that place where the body of Christ is being built up in corporate fellowship. The Church is the community of the faithful, a community with distinctive self-consciousness and a distinctive mission. It is called to fulfil the purposes of God revealed in Jesus Christ and it can only do this by incorporating itself as a witnessing organism.

This incorporation, however, is not a deliberate or considered creation of men who are intent to establish a new church or devise better practices of worship. They themselves have nothing to offer God. They gather in response to the leading of God's own Spirit. They are the *ecclesia* — the "called out." The initiative throughout has been taken by God. God has spoken and God has acted in Jesus Christ.

It was this realization that brought the first Christians together for corporate worship. Early Christian worship was the believers' response in word and deed to God's call and God's act. In the continuance of the action that was begun in the upper room the believers discovered a dimension of spiritual reality that far transcended anything formerly experienced in traditional worship practices, whether of the temple or of the synagogue. Present to the worship experience of the primitive church were the elements that have come to characterize every great tradition in Christian worship. Dr. Joseph Sittler has listed them as five in number: Recollection, Thanksgiving, Participation, Proclamation, and Expectation.[1]

---

[1] From an address "The Shape of the Church's Response in Worship" given by Dr. Joseph Sittler at the North American Conference on Faith and Order at Oberlin, Ohio, September 1957.

You will note that these are all words of action finding expression in movement, speech, song, and ceremony. . . . Recollection engenders thanksgiving which is expressed by the congregation in acts of praise, prayer, repentance, dedication, offering. . . . By and through Word and Sacrament, the congregation *participates* in the Christian Event. They recognize themselves as truly members of the Body of Christ. They are new creatures in Christ.[2]

Oscar Cullmann, writing of the significance of the Lord's Supper in the worship of the primitive Christian community states:

The whole celebration is directed towards this climax, where Christ comes in the Spirit to his own. . . . All the different elements are subordinated to this purpose, which attains its peak in the "coming of Christ" in the Lord's Supper.[3]

This "coming of Christ in the Spirit to his own" is seen by the worshipper to fit into the tradition and expectation of sacred Scripture as its logical and significant fulfilment.

God who at sundry times and in divers manners spake in time past unto the fathers by the prophets, hath in these last days spoken unto us by his Son, whom he hath appointed heir of all things.[4]

This event, this coming of God to men, is related both to its historical context in Scripture and tradition and to the new obligations of Christian discipleship which those who have been called must assume. Thus the reading of the Scriptures and exhortation and preaching become an integral and essential part of the Church's worship. Writing of the practices of the church at Corinth, Professor James Moffatt stated:

It was still the ministry of the Word by inspired apostles, prophets, teachers and catechists which formed the invigorating and authoritative service of worship. The Church met to hear and understand this Word (1 Cor. 14:36), which bound them to God and to one another. . . . The central pulse of the whole service beat in spoken word and testimony

[2] This statement is from a comment by E. S. Frey on Dr. Sittler's analysis of the elements of worship as it appeared in a mimeographed abstract of "The Glory for Which We Build" which was sent out from The Lutheran Church House, 231 Madison Avenue, New York, in 1960.

[3] Oscar Cullmann, *Early Christian Worship*, S.C.M. Press, pp. 20, 26.

[4] Hebrews 1: 1, 2.

upon the distinctive mysteries of the Gospel (14:19) which the love feast represented realistically as a symbol of fellowship.[5]

In the service of worship of the primitive church these two basic elements, the ministry of the word of God and the sacrament of the Lord's Supper, together constitute a theological unity that defies the attempt to isolate either one from the other. The Lord's Supper was administered as the explicit expression of the Gospel which the Church had been called to preach, and the heart of worship was the declaration of the Gospel which both word and sacrament expressed. Only a person versed in the Gospel and, through it, related to Christ and his Church, partook of the Lord's Supper.

This unity of word and sacrament and the intensely intimate and corporate nature of the fellowship is admirably set forth in this oft-quoted passage from the first *Apology* of Justin, which dates from around the middle of the second Christian century:

On the day called Sunday there is a meeting in one place of those who live in cities or the country, and the memoirs of the apostles or the writings of the prophets are read as long as time permits. When the reader has finished, the president in a discourse urges and invites us to the imitation of these noble things. Then we all stand up and offer prayers. And, as said before, when we have finished the prayer, bread is brought, and wine and water, and the president similarly sends up prayers and thanksgivings to the best of his ability, and the congregation assents, saying the Amen; the distribution and reception of the consecrated (elements) by each one, takes place and they are sent by the deacons to the absent. Those who prosper, and who so wish, contribute, each one as much as he chooses to. What is collected is deposited with the president, and he takes care of orphans and widows, and those who are in want on account of sickness or any other cause, and those who are in bonds, and the strangers who are sojourners among (us), and briefly, he is protector of all those in need. We all hold this common gathering on Sunday, since it is the first day, on which God transforming darkness and matter made the universe, and Jesus Christ our Saviour rose from the dead on the same day.[6]

---

[5] James Moffatt, *The First Epistle to the Corinthians,* Harper and Brothers, 1938, pp. xxiii, xiv.

[6] Quoted from *Early Christian Fathers,* ed. Cyril C. Richardson, Westminster, p. 287.

It must be confessed that this picture of early Christian worship that I have drawn and that Justin has described in his apology is an idealized one. It is quite apparent from a reading of Paul's letters to the Corinthians and from other early Christian sources that the actual state of affairs in the congregations was sometimes far removed from this ideal. Nevertheless this picture remains the criterion or norm by which the Church's life and work is to be judged. All that the Church stands for must be seen in the light of this concept of fellowship in Christ. Disunity, for example, about which the apostle had much to say, is a sin simply because it violates this sense of Christian community. The fault with the Corinthians is not that they have a false view of church polity and organization and authority, some of them preferring the wisdom of Apollos to the authority of Paul, but that in thus setting the leaders of the Church against each other they are rending the body of Christ. Paul and Apollos themselves are nothing, only Christ in whom the Church is rooted and from whom it is branched.

This understanding of the Church as a corporate fellowship that nurtures itself through a shared ministry of word and sacrament is essential to an appreciation of its developing worship practices in the first centuries of the Christian era. I have considered it at some length in order to underline the fact that Christian worship at the outset was not a conceptualized thing arising out of some preconceived idea of what worship ought to be but was experiential and real, making its own terms of reference and creating its own indigenous forms.

Increasingly it is being recognized, at least in circles of Christian theology, that the principles of Christian worship are not to be found, as the philosophical idealism of Hegel and the religious romanticism of Schleiermacher implied, either in a study of the development of religions or in the epiphenomena of moral and mystical experience, but in the specific content or datum of the New Testament faith. Recognition of this fact has a significant bearing upon our appreciation of Christian worship practices. The late Principal Richard Davidson of Emmanuel College, Toronto, used to emphasize that the "norm" or standard of a service of Christian worship is not the classic vision recorded in Isaiah

6:1-8: "I saw the Lord sitting upon a throne high and lifted up, and his train filled the temple. Above it stood the seraphims," etc, but the "liturgy of the Upper Room"[7] which expresses the action of an intensely self-conscious community that gathers not to *feel* something but to *do* something. The vision of Isaiah 6 with its magnificent sweep embracing the moods of adoration, confession, penitence and consecration is universal in its religious appeal and is of timeless practical worth in the ordering of a service of public worship which must embrace these moods and experiences. But, valuable and helpful as it is, it does not provide the norm for a Christian worship service. Christian worship, at least in its New Testament expression, is based upon the fact of communion between self-conscious human beings who know and communicate with each other because they know and are known of Jesus Christ.

In saying this I do not mean to imply that early Christian worship was carried on in an environment that was emotionally barren or that the Christian faith at the outset lacked those elements of mystery and awe that are almost universally characteristic of worship experiences. Far from it! The feeling of mystery and wonder was uppermost in the experience of the first Christians. They never got over the wonder of it! But the wonder was related to the specific truth of the revelation in Jesus Christ, the wonder of his reincarnation, his indwelling in the Church which had become his body.

It is natural and logical that students of architecture in taking a historical approach to the study of church building should put their subject in the context of the general field of religious design and should come to a consideration of church building after having first studied religious architecture in its earlier expressions -- the achievements of the Egyptians in building their tombs, the Assyrians and the Greeks their temples, the Jews their synagogues. Valid as this approach may be to the subject of the development of religious architecture in general, it sheds no light on the beginnings of Christian church architecture as such. These beginnings are not found in architectural antecedents, not even those of the synagogue,

---

[7] *The Living Church,* ed. H. W. Vaughan, Toronto, Ryerson Press, p. 99.

but in the practical needs of an esoteric fellowship that was constrained to come together by the expectation of Christ's presence with them.

Just because the worship practices of the Church were determined not by "worship principles" but by the congregation's needs, the matter of the physical environment did not present itself as an architectural and an aesthetic problem. The last thing that the early church wanted to do was to set up a Committee on Church Architecture, or even a Committee on Worship and Ritual! The motto of the first Christians was not "Worship the Lord in the beauty of Holiness!" but *Maranatha* — "Even so, Come, Lord Jesus!" The end was at hand! He who was now with them in the Spirit was soon to return on the clouds of heaven and establish his own kind of rule and reign. In the new Jerusalem no church building would be needed because he would be all in all.

The likelihood, indeed, is that the early Christians, as they gathered for their shared ministry of word and sacrament, did not think of themselves as worshipping in any formal sense at all. Their formal worship was provided in the synagogues and at the temple, and as devout Jews they simply continued to observe the time-honoured worship practices of their religion. Believing that Jesus was the fulfilment of the law and the prophets, they saw nothing inconsistent in worshipping formally in the synagogue and then betaking themselves to their homes for their own more esoteric practices. They even hoped eventually to be able to persuade their fellow Jews to accept Jesus as the Christ and thus relate the Christian revelation to historic Jewish worship practices. A reading of the book of the Acts[8] shows that the apostles made a deliberate attempt to do this. Saul of Tarsus immediately after his conversion "preached Christ in the synagogues that he is the Son of God" (Acts 9:20), and in doing so apparently followed the pattern which the apostles had tried to fix. Even in Gentile territory the mission of the Church "to the Jew first and also to the Greek" was made in and through the synagogues wherever it was possible.

But while as devout Jews the members of the Church continued to worship in their accustomed way they found that as experimental Christians

---

[8] Acts 13:5, 14ff.; 14:1; 17:1, 17, 18.

they had to take themselves aside for the inward renewal of life and for the sharing of that fellowship which the new life in Christ had opened for them. After the doors of the synagogue had finally closed against them they saw that their practices, patterned after the fellowship of the upper room, would have to constitute the totality of their Christian worship. They realized that everything they had hitherto regarded as significant to their worship must now be set within the framework of the experience which the upper room represented. And so, deprived of the use of the synagogues and finding that its Lord "tarried" in his coming, the primitive church established itself as a worshipping fellowship in the homes of its members and developed practices and forms that were true to its genius as the corporate body of Christ.

The very fact that for the first century and a half of the Church's existence the homes of its members seem to have served admirably the practical requirements of worship speaks volumes for the nature of primitive Christian worship and the type of physical accommodation that was best suited to it. Dom Gregory Dix is authority for the statement that the domestic quarters of its members not only adequately served the purposes of early Christian worship but even enhanced it as no rented or public quarters could have done.

It was this originally domestic spirit of Christian worship as much as anything else that preserved the clear understanding of its corporate nature.[9]

Domestic architecture, he insists, was not an unfortunate accommodation to the needs of the early church but the most felicitous expression of its needs.

When, therefore, I say that the development of an architecture did not present itself to the early church as an aesthetic and artistic problem, I do not mean to imply that the physical environment of early Christian worship is not of very great interest and significance. The paradoxical fact is that the key to the architectural requirements of Christian worship is provided by the fact that the early church felt that the need was obviated.

---

[9] Gregory Dix, *The Shape of the Liturgy*, p. 18.

The Church penetrated at the outset to the basic function and form of its worship. It was meeting for a shared ministry of word and sacrament. The problem of finding a place for such a ministry did not arise because the only space available was of the type that best suited the needs of this esoteric fellowship. Where better to meet than in the homes of it devoted and trusted members?

Domestic architecture, therefore, rather than religious architecture, marks the point of departure for our study of the physical requirements, and to this study we shall now briefly turn our attention.

3

The Church
in the Home

The First Epistle to the Corinthians closes with a personal greeting from Aquila and Priscilla who "salute you much in the Lord, with the church that is in their house." In Colossians reference is made to "Nymphas, and the church which is in his house." In the Epistle to Philemon the greetings are extended to "Archippus our fellow-soldier, and to the church in thy house." It would seem clear from these and other references that the church of apostolic days was a church that made its abode in the homes of its leading members.

We may take it that the first services were held in rather insignificant surroundings. At the outset "not many mighty, not many noble" were called to the fellowship. As the Church grew and attracted people of affluence to its ranks larger and more imposing homes would become available to the worshippers.

Dom Gregory Dix in his *Shape of the Liturgy* assumes that in the second century homes of wealthy Roman citizens were open to Christian worship, and he accepts as the norm for second-century worship the setting of a "typical" Roman nobleman's house. (*Figure 1*)

In this plan a vestibule with its door at the street led to the *atrium*, or pillared hall, at the far end of which was a raised platform called the *tablinum*. Behind this platform were the private apartments of the household and the domestic quarters. On the platform itself might be found the sacred hearth which had once been revered as the family shrine. The chair of the head of the house, the *paterfamilias*, occupied the central place on the platform. Immediately below the platform was a large stone table called the *cartibulum* which served various purposes of the household. Farther back in the atrium was the cistern or *impluvium* which furnished the domestic water supply.

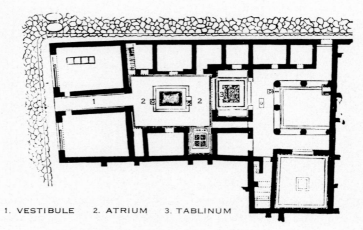

1. VESTIBULE   2. ATRIUM   3. TABLINUM

Figure 1. Plan of the so-called House of the
Tragic Poet.
A typical Roman nobleman's house.

In this plan, states Dix, there was ready to hand everything that the Church needed for its worship. The chair on the platform was the logical place for the president or bishop to sit. The stone table below it served the needs of the eucharistic meal. The pool was available for baptism. On the step, or *gradus*, the soloist or leader of praise would stand. Hence the name "gradual" for the oldest chant of the liturgy, the psalm between the epistle and the Gospel lections.

Although Gregory Dix's picture is attractive, I question whether we ought to accept these arrangements uncritically. Everything sounds a little too convenient to be convincing. Archaeological discoveries of the last fifty or sixty years have shown that there were styles of domestic architecture in the Mediterranean world at that time having little in common with the plan described above, and it is highly improbable that the worship of the early church was almost invariably conducted in such surroundings. In Acts 20:7-12, for example, we are shown early Christian worship in a vastly different domestic setting.

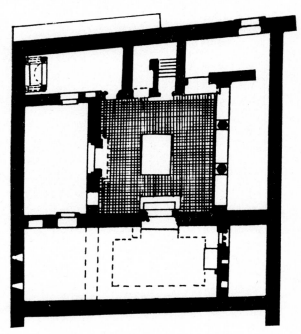

Figure 2. Plan of House-church, Dura-Europos.

These reservations do not invalidate Dix's main contention. What he is pleading for is recognition of the intensely corporate nature of early Christian worship. The Church is the "household of God," the *ecclesia,* the "called out." What is done in worship can best be done in a private domestic setting where there is a corporate sharing of the risen life of Christ.

Of no less interest than Dix's plan is that of a house at Dura-Europos on the Euphrates which was constructed at the beginning of the third century. In this eastern building we find preserved the most complete example of a house-church (*Figure 2*). J. G. Davies describes it thus:

Access from the street is obtained by a single entrance door in the north wall which opens into a vestibule and thence into the court. On the east side of the court there is a portico and along the other three five rooms are disposed. In the north west corner is the baptistery, richly decorated with frescoes, its font surmounted by a baldachin. Opposite to this, along the southern wall of the house, two rooms have been made into one, at the east end of which there is a small platform for the altar and a door to the side of it leads into what was originally the sacristy. The use of the other room along the west wall is doubtful, but graffiti suggest that it was employed either as a triclinium or as a class room for the catechumens.[1]

The probability is that a congregation feeling the need for permanent accommodation would lease or buy a home such as the one described above and would make the physical changes that were necessary better to adapt it to worship purposes. What apparently happened in the house at Dura-Europos is that a partition was removed between two rooms to provide a single room large enough for the gathering of the faithful. It appears that a separate chamber was furnished with a baptistery.

This sort of thing was probably done frequently throughout the church, the local needs of the congregations determining the nature of the alterations and renovations that would be made. The congregation would continue to worship in such domestic quarters as long as it could practically do so, and it is reasonable to suppose that when the time came to construct an entirely new building the congregation would adhere fairly closely to this familiar domestic plan.

Just when this time came we cannot say with certainty. The second century was not a propitious one for church building. The persecutions that were then being launched against the sect, even though sporadic and localized, would have discouraged any desire on the part of congregations to erect permanent quarters. It was not until the latter half of the third

---

[1] J. G. Davies, *The Origin and Development of Early Christian Architecture*, S. C. M. Press, London, 1952, p. 20.

century that the church found conditions generally favourable for the erection of permanent church buildings. From the reign of Gallienus to the middle of Diocletian's reign, that is, for a period from about 260 to about 303, the church enjoyed an almost unbroken peace, and it is to that period that we must look for any significant development of church architecture.

There is, however, evidence of some church building early in the third century and even before the close of the second century. The *Chronicle of Arbela,* which dates from about 500, refers to the third Bishop Isaac who presided from 123 to 136 as having been responsible for the building of a church. This reference, however, is based upon a document, the *Record of Abel,* which was allegedly written in the second century but the authenticity of which is open to serious question. It is recorded in the *Chronicle of Edessa* that there was in the city of Edessa in northeast Syria a *templum ecclesiae Christianorum* which was destroyed by a flood in 302. The authenticity of this passage has also been challenged. Tertullian refers to the existence of church buildings in the west in the second century and from his references[2] one would conclude that some of the buildings were fairly elaborate structures. Few traces of second-century buildings remain, however, and any idea of their appearance and furnishings must be largely conjectural.

One has the feeling that much that has been written and said about the environment of worship in this period is largely a reading into the picture of liturgical ideas and convictions that are dear to the beholder. This is the temptation, of course, that confronts one in any phase of the beginnings of Christianity. We are told that it is a basic principle of historical research in the field of liturgics to find the starting point of one's study in later sources and then to trace the way painfully back to earlier days where the sources are few and far between and where development is still going on. The necessity of this method is obvious but so are the dangers. Nothing is more tempting than the desire to fill the gaps of knowledge with theories and opinions that may or may not correspond

---

[2] *De Spect., De Pud.; De Idol.,* vii.

to the actual facts of the case, and to dogmatize about things for which there is no good reason to be dogmatic. We do well to recall the danger and try as best we can to avoid it.

The student of church architecture, fortunately, has an advantage that is denied the liturgist. He can start from a point in time closer to the real beginning of his study than can one who attempts to trace the origin and development of Christian worship practices. The Church was engaged in worship from its earliest days, but for the first century and a half of its existence it did not seriously concern itself with architecture.

All we can say is that the tendencies that produced church building in the late third century were at work much earlier. Dr. Joseph Sittler has remarked that once a congregation has decided to meet at a certain fixed time in a certain fixed place the problem of architecture presents itself.

People build churches. They do that because, in response to the summons and the tasks of the gospel, they must be together. They have to keep the wet rain off their heads, enclose a space to keep out the cold, or the heat, or the noise, arrange the space to sing, speak, listen, worship, teach, behold and participate in a mystery.

But when this much is clear the problem is merely stated; it isn't solved. And if a space is enclosed to provide only for these functions it can't be solved righteously at all.

For this listening is not just to another speech, this singing is no concert or folk-entertainment, this teaching is not an adjunct to general education. There is a difference; and the entire architectural performance will be righteous to the extent that it penetrates to this difference, defines it, and then realizes it in form and material.[3]

The significance of the third century to the study of church architecture lies in the fact that the Christian Church had to do just that. It had to penetrate to an understanding of its role in the imperial world, define it, and then realize it in form and material.

---

[3] From "A hammer, the Incarnation and Architecture" in *The Christian Century*, March 27, 1958.

The house had served admirably as long as the Church continued to think of itself as an esoteric colony of heaven waiting patiently for the end. By the turn of the third century, however, the end had had to be indefinitely postponed and the Church had settled down to face the likelihood of its continuing to exist in a world that had an indefinite future. The Church now found that it had to be the Church no longer in self-conscious isolation and concealment from a hostile world but in active relationship to a society that was challenging it and, in turn, being challenged by it. Persecution had failed to halt the growth of the institution and the imperial world was increasingly puzzled about it. The emperors themselves did not quite know where or how to fit the Church into their imperial schemes. They were not prepared to lavish any favours upon it but they recognized that for political reasons they must deal cautiously with it. The Church for its part had as yet no ends to serve or purposes to achieve other than those intrinsic to its own mission.

It is the writer's conviction that no period of church history is of more practical interest to us than this period immediately prior to the "peace of the Church" so-called. There is, indeed, a striking parallel between the situation confronting the Church at that time and the situation that confronts it today. Today, as then, the status of the Church as a social institution and the significance of its role in society are not too clearly defined. Today, as then, the world does not quite know what to make of this institution that calls itself the body of Christ. Today, as then, the church builder has to fashion his design to meet the needs of an institution that is soberly reappraising its function.

In all this there are implications for church architecture. A congregation standing in the reformed tradition today adheres basically to the principles of worship that informed the Church in the third century, and it is natural to assume that a relationship that exists in liturgy will show itself in architecture as well. It is my conviction that this ought to be the case, and that the church of the late twentieth century can learn much, even in the practical matter of architecture, from the church of the late third century. In saying this I do not mean to suggest that the churches of the twentieth century should attempt to recover any particular style of early Christian architecture, or even go back for inspiration to the forms that characterized that era. Such eclecticism would be manifestly absurd. My contention, rather, is that the Protestant churches today may profitably be guided in their motives by the principles that inspired those forms. It is not possible to study the church architecture of that ancient era without realizing how well it met the Church's theological and liturgical needs. The motives were clear and the expression was sound. The Church was doing what it had to do—no more, no less.

Fortunately the period provides many examples of church building worthy of study. The forty years' peace enjoyed prior to Diocletian's cruel persecution gave the Church its wanted opportunity to build and it seized the opportunity avidly. It is said that in Rome itself there were more than forty church buildings by the turn of the century and that in Nicomedia, the eastern capital, a church could be seen towering in full view of the emperor's palace. Eusebius of Caesarea wrote of

those assemblies thronged with countless men, and the multitudes that gathered together in every city, and the famed concourses in the places of prayer; by reason of which they were no longer satisfied with the buildings of olden times, and would erect from the foundations churches of spacious dimensions throughout all the cities.[4]

The growth of the Christian Church in the late third century was so rapid and widespread that the period may be regarded as formative in the sense of tending to "fix" the architectural pattern that came to characterize the physical design of ancient churches. Diocletian's persecution came half a century too late to do more than temporarily arrest the growth of the Church, and when Constantine issued his Edict of Toleration in 313 the church simply resumed its building programme from the point at which it had left off. Imperial approval and patronage added tremendous stimulus to the programme, of course, but the pattern of the design had already been fixed. For centuries to come the church that "looked like a church" was the building patterned after the basic design of the late third century—the so-called classic basilican style.

---

[4] *H. E.* viii, i.

4

The Basilican Plan

The word basilica comes from a Greek adjective $\beta\alpha\sigma\iota\lambda\iota\kappa\dot{\eta}$, which means "royal" or "regal." Used as a substantive it referred originally to a person attached to the king such as a courtier or someone of the highest excellence. The noun assumed an architectural connotation when it came to be applied to the portico on the agora at Athens in which the archon "basileus" dispensed justice. In Rome it referred to the ingenious system of colonnades that separated a special section of the Forum which was reserved for the transaction of imperial business. In process of time the word came to refer to a distinctive type of building possessed of oblong hall with double colonnade and apse such as was used for general assembly purposes in connection with the law courts or the services of the Christian Church. By Constantine's time the word appears to have acquired a definitely churchly connotation. States Davies:

When Constantine wrote to Macarius of Jerusalem about the projected Church of the Holy Sepulchre, he instructed the bishop to build the finest basilica yet seen, but he did not consider it necessary to give any further details about it, thus intimating that the term $\beta\alpha\sigma\iota\lambda\iota\kappa\dot{\eta}$ was well understood and had a definite connotation.[1]

The question of the origin of the basilica and, in particular, of the influence of the Christian church upon the development of the style is

---

[1] Op. cit., p. 35.

complicated and involved. The theory has recently been revived by Gregory Dix that the Christian basilica developed from the private dwelling and that early church architecture is simply an evolution of domestic requirements. This is a place where the archaeologists can have their field day. Davies' conclusion seems eminently sensible, and we shall leave the matter of the origin and development with him:

Such creations as this do not suddenly spring into existence, they are the fruit of long periods of steady growth and experiment, and the origin of the basilica lies not in the genius of an individual architect, but in the joint endeavours of both pagans and Christians in the first three centuries of the Church's history.[2]

Figure 3.   Plan of S. Apollinare
Nuovo, Ravenna.

The significant fact is that the Christian Church claimed the style for itself and came to employ it almost universally in its service. What the domestic building had been able to provide in the way of worship facilities for the few the basilica was able to provide no less adequately for the many.

There are several types or styles of fourth-century basilica. The most general by far is the Hellenistic type, which was to be found along the coastline of the eastern Mediterranean and throughout central Syria, Asia Minor and parts of north Africa. The plan of S. Apollinare Nuovo at Ravenna may be regarded as typical of this type (see *Figure* 3).

[2] Ibid., p. 16.

From the outside the Hellenistic basilica would be a simple and unimposing structure of undressed brick. Ornamentation would be meagre and would be applied only to the façade. This façade might consist of a high gable corresponding to the peak of the roof or perhaps, if the building were more elaborate, of a screen to conceal the roof. The doorways would probably be given special attention but, for the most part, the building would be austere and unimpressive. The church was not erected to impress the passer-by.

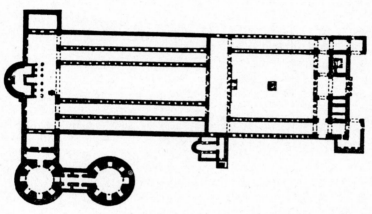

Figure 4. Plan of the first St. Peter's, Rome.

Doors on the street gave access to a vestibule or narthex which led to the main body of the church. In the Hellenistic basilica this vestibule was contained within the main walls of the building and was part of the single structure, separated from the nave only by a screen or narthos (rods).

In the Roman type of basilica, of which the first St. Peter's in Rome may be said to furnish a classic example (see *Figure 4*), there was no enclosed vestibule but rather an open pillared court or atrium adjoining the main body of the church. The function of this court or atrium was identical, however, with that of the Hellenistic narthex. It provided an intermediary place between the sanctuary and the world. Here the inquirers assembled for instruction before being admitted to the mysteries within. Here the needy gathered for alms.

Simple as the third-century plan appears to be, the design was carefully worked out to serve the worship requirements of a congregation of the faithful. These requirements, in the late third century, were still basically the provision of a ministry of word and sacrament in a fellowship of intense intimacy. The early Christian basilica was a truly functional building, serving these requirements well.

The building itself was well-proportioned. Whatever its size, it remained of room proportions, roughly twice as long as it was wide, with side aisles about half the width of the nave. Such a building did not become formidable even after it had become large. Splendid proportions, to which the early builders adhered faithfully, together with the provision of a flat wood ceiling, also assured excellent acoustical effects.

The long lines of the nave, accented by the line of pillars on each side, led the eye to the apse where the action of worship took place. On the platform or bema of the apse, raised several steps above the floor of the nave, was the bishop's chair or cathedra. From this "basilican position," as it came to be called, the bishop or president faced the people surrounded by his presbyters. Below the platform and close to the congregation was the holy table around which the deacons were grouped. In the main body of the church stood the laity, men on one side, women on the other, facing the bishop. We might note in passing that in the pre-Nicene eucharist presbyters and deacons administered the rites, even to the fraction. The only part belonging exclusively to the bishop was the eucharistic prayer.

Walter Lowrie states that the table was movable, and that as the number of clergy increased for special observances the table would be brought further forward. The usual position for the table, however, was on the chord of the apse. In later years it came to be fenced off by a balustrade or "chancel" of marble. States Lowrie:

No one would speak slightingly of the Holy Table as a piece of furniture, since more than anything else it determined the form of the house of the church. Yet in size it was insignificant. It never was enlarged in proportion with the size of the building, but in the immense churches erected after the Peace it retained the size, a size determined only by its use, which had sufficed for the earliest houses of worship. It was almost square, and tradition limited it to something like a yard and a quarter in its greater dimension.[3]

"Holy Table" is the correct designation. For the first four or five centuries the table was regarded consistently as a table and not as an altar. After the sixth century it gradually came to be referred to as the altar, having been enlarged to accommodate the relics of saints and assuming the slab-like appearance which has since characterized it in the liturgical churches.

We have noted that the bishop or president stood on the platform at the centre of the apse to preside over the celebration of the eucharist, and it may be presumed that in the fourth century he preached or exhorted from that position as well. We learn in the *Apostolic Constitutions,* which dates from the second half of the fourth century, that the "ambo" was used for the reading of the lessons, the intimations and sometimes the preaching of the sermon. While the position of this ambo or reading desk was not uniform the most common position for it seems to have been at the front centre of the apse. Ruskin the artist makes a statement concerning pulpit arrangements in the early Church that is not irrelevant to this discussion of fourth century furnishings. Speaking of the unfortunate impression that a central pulpit makes when installed in the apse of an English church in the rightful position of the communion table, he adds:

I nevertheless believe that the Scotch congregations are perfectly right, and have restored the real arrangement of the primitive churches. The chevalier Bunsen informed me lately, that, in all the early basilicas he has examined, the LATERAL PULPITS are of more recent date than the rest of the building; that he knows of none placed in the position which they now occupy, both in the basilicas and gothic churches, before the ninth century; and that there can be no doubt that the bishop always preached or exhorted, in the primitive times, from his throne in the centre of the apse, the altar always being set at the centre of the church . . . . His Excellency found by experiment in Santa Maria Maggiore, the largest of the Roman basilicas, that the voice could be heard more plainly from the centre of the apse than from any other spot in the whole church.[4]

---

[3] Walter Lowrie, *Art in the Early Church,* New York, Pantheon Press, p. 118.
[4] Quoted from A. L. Drummond, *The Church Architecture of Protestantism,* p. 206.

Of this primitive arrangement, however, there are no physical reminders. In most of the reconstructions of basilican churches the pulpit has been given a lateral position extending well out into the nave, usually to one side of the marble rail enclosing the altar. That there is good precedent, however, in the furnishings of the early church, for retaining a central pulpit *behind* the communion table is not open to question.

The primitive church was vigorously opposed, on religious grounds, to the use of pictorial arts, and this prejudice or conviction was not easily overcome. It is astonishing to recall how many leaders of the Church, men of the character and influence of Basil, the two Gregories and Chrysostom, remained opposed to the religious use of pictures and other visual arts. In 315 the bishops and presbyters assembled at the Synod of Elvira in Spain unanimously condemned the use of religious pictures, declaring that "there should be no pictures in the church building, lest what is worshipped and adored might be painted on the walls."[5] Even as late as the fifth century Jerome was dubious about art, and Augustine himself refers to its seductions.

We may assume therefore that the pre-Nicene basilicas were sparingly decorated. The art used would be symbolic rather than realistic, and would be confined largely to surface decoration. Emblems such as the ship, the fish, the grape, the alpha and the omega, and various forms of the cross would be in evidence.

It was probably the recognition of the innocuous nature of sepulchral art, that is, the decorations used in the burial places in the catacombs, that prepared the way for a more general acceptance of art in the church buildings. In the Christian cemeteries the hope of everlasting life, from very early days, found expression in simple but vivid frescoes depicting symbols of everlasting life, and scenes from both the Old Testament and the Christian writings. The wide extent to which this kind of art was used in the catacombs suggests that the rank and file of believers did not share

---

[5] Quoted from a translation from the Latin of Canon 36 by Walter Lowrie as it appears on page 29 of *Art in the Early Church*.

the distrust of art which the official position of the Church represented. The question of how extensively art was used in the churches of the early fourth century must remain open.

After Constantine's time, however, the restraints were removed and the Church, at least in those assignments where the emperors were able to have their way, went all out for colour and adornment. Constantine's successors lavished untold wealth upon the great churches, both of the East and the West. Rome, Constantinople, Jerusalem, and Antioch vied with each other in the erection of fanes worthy of the Lord of heaven. The elaborate and skilful development of architecture in the fifth and sixth centuries, with the flat roof of the basilica forsaken for a series of aspiring domes, provided incomparable scope for mosaic work and the display of surface decorations. Imperial patronage, a sympathetic environment and the noblest of all themes, together with an enduring medium, enabled the craftsmen to endow the churches of the Empire with a legacy of mosaics the glories of which have not faded to this day. In the lines of Thomson the poet,

> the pillar'd Dome, magnific, heav'd
> Its ample Roof; and Luxury within
> Pour'd out her glittering Stores.

Paul Tillich has said that for him "what no amount of study of church history has brought about was accomplished by the mosaics in ancient Roman basilicas."[6]

The greatest of them all was the Haggia Sophia in Constantinople, built under Justinian in the sixth century. If the old chroniclers are to be believed, it was the celebration of the Liturgy of Saint Chrysostom in this great church that resulted in the conversion of Russia to Orthodox Christianity in the tenth century.

The envoys of the Grand Duke Vladimir, sent to the west to search for a new religion, were present at the celebration of the Eucharist by the Patriarch in the presence of the Emperor in Saint Sophia. On their return

[6] Paul Tillich, *The Interpretation of History*, p. 16.

to Kieff they reported "We no longer knew whether we were on earth or in heaven, we saw such beauty and magnificence that we knew not how to tell it."[7]

What must be added is that this glorious development of Byzantine architecture and the perfection of mosaic art, about which so much has been learned in recent years, signifies more to the student of church history than merely an interesting development in the field of the arts. What is involved here is a changing conception of the nature of the Church and the function of its public worship. The manner in which the church of the fourth century embraced the arts and elaborated its architecture reflects a subtle departure from the basic concept of worship which the early church had held.

We have seen that the worship of the primitive and the pre-Nicene church required for its expression an environment creating a feeling of spiritual intimacy. A sense of community was present to the experience of common worship which after Constantine's time came increasingly to be lost. James Hastings Nichols has stated that in the absence in congregations of the fourth and fifth centuries of a sense of conscious community "the sacraments were less to celebrate, than to create a sense of mystical brotherhood. This called for a great elaboration of liturgy and architectural magnificence and every conceivable accessory to create a mood of participation in a mystical body so conspicuously contrasted to social and ethical realities."[8] Worship was becoming increasingly a spectacle, and the primary function of architecture and the churchly arts was to create a sense of supernatural mystery which acts psychologically upon the worshipper.

The mystical experience that murals or mosaics are to help invoke within the faithful is emphatically not of this world; the celestial vision depicted is to make us forget that we find ourselves in a building of stone or mortar, since inwardly we have entered the heavenly sanctuary.[9]

The responsibility for effecting this subtle change in the concept of worship cannot be laid entirely to Constantine and to his successors. The

[7] James Hastings Nichols, *Primer for Protestants,* New York, Association Press, 1951, p. 30.

[8] Loc. cit.

[9] Otto von Simpson, *The Gothic Cathedral,* Pantheon Books, 1959, p. 9.

Church itself had come to look at things differently. The fact of the matter was that the Lord had not returned in the manner in which the primitive church had expected him to return. The world still remained and it looked as if it was going to remain. This was the world in which, for the time being at least, the kingdom of heaven was going to have to be realized. The imperial world, increasingly, was being fashioned into a Christian realm with earthly rulers themselves acknowledging the existence of the kingdom of heaven upon this earth. The theme in the apse mosaics at Ravenna and elsewhere of the emperor as the appointed representative of God asserting his divine as well as his imperial dominion admirably illustrates the sense of mission under which church and state jointly governed the affairs of men. In the material realm what higher task could emperors and prelates give themselves than the task of endowing the world with fanes that could properly be called worthy dwellings for Him who had taken to Himself His great power and was reigning in the kingdoms of men?

To fashion his design for this purpose now became the architectural assignment of the church builder, who sought to build and adorn his church for the greater glory of God. How admirably he succeeded in doing this is seen not only in the Byzantine art and architecture at which we have briefly glanced but more particularly in the Gothic architecture of the middle ages.

5

Worship
without Communion

We have seen that after the third century a significant change came over the worship practices of the Christian Church and that liturgy and architecture developed forms that took the Church ever further from the earlier environment of its worship. This development was, of course, gradual, and liturgists sometimes refer to it as evolutionary, pointing out the manner in which the necessities of worship gradually brought these changes to pass.

The fact that the changes were gradual should not, however, obscure the fact that a basic distinction exists between the worship of the early church and that of later centuries. Our concern is to appreciate the nature of these changes and to try to measure the extent to which they mark a defection or a departure from the principles that ordered the worship of the primitive church.

In the year 313 the two emperors Licinius and Constantine declared: "We grant to the Christians and to all others full liberty of following that religion which each may choose."[1] These two edicts, which some have called the Magna Carta of Christianity, are among the most important documents in the history of mankind. While Constantine did not formally adopt Christianity as the religion of the state he saw that it was capable of becoming the great unifying bond of the empire and he personally

---

[1] L. P. Qualben, *A History of the Christian Church,* Thomas Nelson and Sons, New York, 1940, p. 116.

encouraged its growth and influence. As Christianity swept on its triumphal way the forces of paganism fell before it and the Church took to itself those elements of the culture which it was capable of assimilating and using to its own advantage. The extent to which pagan religious practices of the Graeco-Roman world influenced the Christian liturgy during the fourth century and afterwards is a moot point, but there is no question that the Church adapted itself to the spirit and temper of an age that loved pageantry and display. Dramatic elements were incorporated into the ritual of the Church which, from the western point of view, make the service appear heavy and overgrown.

This dramatization of worship, however, must be seen in the light of the sympathies of the times. It is no criticism of the Church to say that the formal expression of its worship was altered by its pagan environment. Cultural adaptation is as inevitable as it is desirable in the growth of a living organism, and the challenge that confronts the Church in every age is the challenge to make itself indigenous to its culture without compromising its nature. The Greeks of the Mediterranean world, then as now, loved display and formality, and to the extent that this dramatization of worship in the post-Nicene period represented a realistic sharing by all the people in the action of worship it must be recognized as a natural evolution rather than as a perversion of early Christian worship. While subtle dangers no doubt attend the use of the dramatic and the spectacular in worship it is a misconception to suppose that an impoverished order of service is necessarily closer to the primitive norm than an embellished one.

More serious was the danger that lay in the growing tendency to mystery that exalted the priest and increasingly set him and his office apart from the fellowship of the worshipping people. In process of time the clergy came to be conceived as a special order separated from the laity both by their official capacity which included extensive legal jurisdiction inside and outside the church and also, as it was believed, by higher religious and moral gifts which were of an indelible character. A peculiar numinous quality attached itself to the clergy—a kind of special holiness that could not really be shared by the people. The clergy, placed in a class by themselves, found it easy to withdraw from the fellowship of common worshippers and to concentrate on the higher mysteries of their office. Needless to say this preoccupation of the clergy with the higher mysteries of their calling worked to the disadvantage of both a pulpit and a pastoral ministry. It would be difficult to picture a worship service after the fifth century into which the preaching of an Augustine or a Chrysostom would have fitted.

This functional dislocation, if we may call it that, may be seen architecturally in the provision of the veil or screen that came eventually to separate the action of the worshipper from the action of the priests. In the fourth century there was introduced into Syria, it seems, a kind of curtain or veil which hid the "sanctuary" from the laity. When this veil came to be developed into an elaborate iconostasis it served to underline very effectively the separation between higher clergy and deacons and laity. "As often as I worship in a Greek Cathedral," wrote the late Professor William Malcolm Macgregor in a facetious vein, "and watch the service being carried through afar off, and but dimly heard, always what occurs to me is this, 'So the veil of the temple has been stitched together again'."[2]

The most serious development, however, lay neither in the elaboration of ritual nor in the functional dislocation of the clergy but in a later development that saw the central element of Christian worship, the shared fellowship of the Lord's Supper, transformed into a "thearcic mystery" into which only the celebrating priest himself could wholly enter. This change of communion into Mass was well on its way in the post-Nicene period, but it became part of the official doctrine of the western church only in the eighth century. In the year 750 John of Damascus refused to allow "elements after consecration to be called types or symbols of the body and blood, since consecration effects a fundamental change in them."[3] It was asserted that the miracle of the

---

[2] W. M. Macgregor, *The Making of a Preacher,* The Westminster Press, Philadelphia, p. 16.
[3] Quoted by E. S. Freeman in *The Lord's Supper in Protestantism,* p. 51.

Mass, specifically performed by the priest, transforms the elements of bread and wine into the actual blood and body of Christ and endows them with supernatural powers. Christ's presence is realized no longer in the corporate fellowship of the Church which is his body, but in the spectacular act, rightly performed, of the officiating priest duly authorized to perform it.

The ideas of the Supper as a symbol of the fellowship of believers with one another and their living Lord, as a dramatic commemoration of his atoning sacrifice, and as a vivid reminder of his spiritual presence gave way entirely to the idea of a priestly sacrifice. Once that idea was given full sway, the whole priestly system of medieval Christianity followed logically. And that marked the ultimate elimination of such characteristics of evangelical worship as spontaneity, evangelistic preaching of the gospel, committal of life to Christ under the influence of the Spirit, and congregational participation.[4]

The congregation itself came to have no liturgical function. It was there simply to behold the miracle of the Mass and to receive its benefits. "Heave it higher, Sir Priest!" was the demand of the medieval layman, shouted from the nave, when he had difficulty seeing the host at the consecration. All that mattered was that he see what had transpired at the celebration and receive the visible assurance that the "Presence" had been "realized." Quite secondary if not actually antithetical to the spirit of medieval Catholic worship were the considerations that had determined the function of a church building of the early third century — the creation of a community of spiritual fellowship through the participation of all the worshippers in a shared ministry of word and sacrament.

The monumental achievements of medieval art and architecture represent primarily the adaptation of the Church's physical environment to this kind of liturgical necessity. Since Gothic in its full-flowering most admirably serves these needs, Gothic architecture to be rightly understood must be seen against the background of the liturgical changes which were wrought in the west after the eighth century.

---

[4] Ilion T. Jones, *A Historical Approach to Evangelical Worship,* Abingdon, New York, pp. 112, 113.

It has become the custom in our time, especially among architects, to "explain" the Gothic achievement in terms either of economic necessity or structural determinism, pointing out the manner in which factors such as the shortage of labour and the lack of stone forced the builders to move away from the massive Roman type to a more delicate style of architecture. The fact is, however, that in the region where Gothic achieved its early eminence, namely in the Isle de France, such considerations did not apply. It was liturgical rather than economic and structural necessity that brought St. Denis and, later, Chartres into being. In his scholarly and sympathetic study, *The Gothic Cathedral,* Professor Otto von Simpson develops the thesis that Gothic architecture "in the solemn language of its form" was the deliberate creation of an awe-inspiring environment that would most significantly enhance medieval worship. According to the early medieval mystics and other writers true beauty is anchored in metaphysical reality. This reality can be expressed and recreated through visible and audible harmonies which music and architecture and the arts supply. Contemplation of such harmonies leads the worshipping soul directly to the experience of God. Majestic and impressive as the development of Byzantine and Romanesque art and architecture had been, what was needed to satisfy medieval religious experience was a more luminous, a more ethereal style, structures less earth-bound than the heavy buildings of the Roman Empire. Twelfth-century Gothic provided the answer. Soaring arches and great expanses of shimmering glass created that luminous atmosphere in which the mysterious spectacle of the Mass could be set forth most majestically.

The plan of the building itself and the relationship of the parts clearly bespeak this medieval function. Significant is the absence of narthex or fore-court. In the early Christian basilica this place of preparation was considered essential to the plan of a church. In the medieval Gothic building, however, no such intermediary place was provided or needed. The worshipper was simply thrust into the building through a narrow porch at the west end or more frequently through doors in transepts at the sides. The nave itself is the separated area of the church and people can do their coming and their going in it, exposing themselves to the subtle influences of the awesome environment. Somewhere in the nave, either near the crossing or farther down, is the pulpit where the priest may exhort the people. This pulpit, however, is not a part of the sanctuary, and preaching, if any there be, is not properly part of the action of medieval worship. To the "east" of the crossing is the rood screen giving access to a raised platform which was technically called the *pulpitum*. Beyond this chancelled area so-called was the quire whose stalls were reserved for the clergy. Beyond this on a further elevation was the sanctuary proper—a railed area enclosing the altar where the crowning act of worship took place.

If one accepts the medieval conviction that the function of church architecture and the churchly arts is to create a mood and an environment fitting for the re-enactment of a mysterious and dramatic spectacle, the adequacy of twelfth-century Gothic is not open to question. As an instrument of mood-creation it has never been improved upon and perhaps never will. Paraphrasing the words of our Lord with reference to the greatness of John the Baptist we can say that of architectural styles evolved by men there has not arisen a greater than medieval Gothic.

But worship of this kind obviously belongs to an environment vastly different from that of the action of third-century worship, and it goes without saying that the architectural forms that were developed for medieval Catholic worship are not entirely congenial to a body of people which adheres to the principles and practices of primitive and early Christianity. This fact was being made abundantly clear to the Church of Rome long before the full impact of the Protestant Reformation came to be felt. Long before the time of Martin Luther protests were being registered across the Church against the abuses of its worship, and individuals and congregations in widely separated places were attempting to reform worship practices. The Lollards in England, the Hussites in Bohemia and the Waldenses in Italy were trying to recover a concept of communion that would involve the participation of all who belonged to the household of faith and that would, they believed, be truer to the command of Christ than the priestly rites of the Mass.

It is not surprising that these attempts to reform medieval worship were inspired by men — laymen for the most part — who had been able to expose themselves to a study of the New Testament Scriptures and had come to see how far removed from the beliefs and practices of primitive Christianity was the worship of their day. What Martin Luther did was to make articulate the convictions of an ever-growing number of men and women who felt that something was radically wrong with the Church. It was inevitable that when the storm broke its force should strike most directly against the abuses of worship and that architecture and the arts should feel the direct impact of this protest. After all, liturgy is simply what the people do in their worship, and if the people come to the conviction that what they are doing is wrong they will seize upon drastic and sweeping remedies to make themselves right in the sight of God.

6

The Protestant
Reformation

Hard upon the reform of the Church in the sixteenth century came striking changes in the physical environment of worship. These changes were conditioned by local circumstances and were inspired by varied and mixed motives. Economic, political and sociological circumstances all had a bearing upon the situation, and the impact of the Protestant Reformation on church architecture was felt far more forcefully in some situations than in others.

In Germany, the home of the Protestant Reformation, the picture was confused. Luther's primary concern had been to reform the Church's faith and practice. His liturgical projects were, therefore, mainly revisions of the Catholic Mass, and he retained in public worship many practices of medieval Catholicism that were not in his opinion actually contrary to New Testament teaching. Many of the church buildings in Germany were left virtually untouched, and Romish elements were retained both in liturgy and in architecture that would have been intolerable, say, to a Swiss Calvinist or to a Scottish Presbyterian.

This sympathy of the Lutheran Church with Roman Catholic practices was perhaps more apparent than real, however, and even in those churches where the traditional Catholic arrangements were retained the focus of worship was transferred from the crucifix and the pyx to the open Bible. In the seventeenth century, when new Lutheran churches came to be built following the ravages of the Thirty Years' War, radical changes were made in church design. In these new buildings the pulpit and altar, the font and the organ were all grouped closely together so that the people could see and hear what was happening and participate together in the worship. Most of these seventeenth-century buildings in Germany were of simple rectangular shape, although some were oval or round. The pulpit was invariably placed high in the front centre of the church with the altar immediately below it close to the congregation.

In Switzerland there was no compromise with pre-Reformation practices. John Calvin was not in the least concerned with reforming the Roman liturgy but was determined simply to recover the purity of the Gospel. If the logic of this attempt meant the rejection of a thousand years' tradition and the removal of the Church's artistic treasures, Calvin was prepared to pay the price. Nothing was to be said or done in worship that was not *in accordance with* Scripture. This is not to imply that Calvin was a negative reformer. He was actually a great lover of the arts and was sympathetic to their right religious use. But he refused to allow any work of man's hands to assume a mediatorial function. Man's reliance for salvation was to be placed on the pure Gospel alone. "I wish for a pure and legitimate use of both (sculpture and painting)," he declared in his *Institutes,* "lest those things which the Lord hath conferred on us for His glory and our benefit, be not only corrupted by preposterous abuse, but even perverted to our own ruin" — a statement that sounds reminiscent of the declaration of the bishops at the Council of Elvira in the fourth century.

The architectural setting for reformed worship in Switzerland, accordingly, was a simple "meeting house" where minister and people might gather in a spirit of intimacy for a shared ministry of word and sacrament. We emphasize word *and* sacrament, because Calvin's desire was that the Lord's Supper should provide the regular diet of worship. He labelled the separation of word from sacrament as "our corrupt practice" and strove, vainly as it worked out, for a weekly observance of the Lord's Supper.

"In other expressions of the Reformation," states Marvin S. Halverson, "the entire building became the sanctuary as the belief in the priesthood of all believers extended participation in the liturgy to the entire people."[1] In Holland, where Calvinist doctrine had made a profound impression upon the people, the churches were shorn of their medieval adornments. The walls were whitewashed and the windows filled with clear glass. Invariably the pulpit gained the place of attention in these revamped buildings.

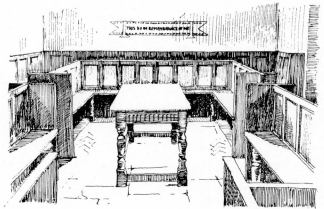

Figure 5. English pre-Laudian chancel, Hayle, Cheltenham.

Similar changes followed in Scotland where Calvinist doctrine was enthusiastically embraced. The first church built in Scotland after the Reformation, St. Cuthbert's of Bruntisland, which was erected in the year 1592, was designed in the shape of a Greek cross with the great pulpit thrust well out into the nave of the church. In front of this pulpit was a large table around which the congregation gathered for the celebration of the Lord's Supper.

In England the Book of Common Prayer had laid down that the services of the Church should be acts of worship in which the congregation

---

[1] "Getting Good Architecture For the Church" in *The Architectural Record*, December, 1956, p. 133.

as well as the clergy plays a part. In the Articles of Religion of the Anglican Church the visible Church is defined as a "congregation of faithful men, in which the pure Word of God is preached, and the sacraments (be) duly administered according to Christ's ordinance, in all those things that of necessity are requisite to the same." This Protestant concept of the Church and its public worship called for a radical revision of architecture. Fortunately the expiry of Gothic architecture coincident with the coming of the Reformation helped to make that possible. Church builders no longer felt themselves restricted to a style that was associated primarily with the medieval point of view. As a result hardly any Gothic churches were built in England after 1543 — the date of the secession of the Church of England from Rome — until Gothic revived itself again two hundred years later (*Figure 5*).

When Martin Bucer found refuge in England after being driven out of Germany he was able to promote liturgical ideas that had already been effectively put into practice in reformed churches on the Continent. Bucer started from the premise that the congregation should be able both to understand and to share in Christian worship. The logic of this conviction, applied to church building on the Continent, had been the removal of the altar from the far east end of the church down into the nave. Upon Bucer's suggestion the same change was made in many English parish churches.[2]

In the seventeenth century William Laud, who became Archbishop of Canterbury, reacted violently against these Protestant changes and attempted to restore the medieval arrangement of furnishings, particularly with regard to the location of the altar. The body of opinion which he represented failed of conviction, however, and he himself paid dearly for his Romish sympathies.

---

[2] A detailed study of some of the changes that were made to medieval buildings in England at this time is provided in G. W. O. Addleshaw and Frederick Etchells' splendid book, *The Architectural Setting of Anglican Worship,* a study of which would do much to correct popular misconceptions concerning Anglican worship practices after the Reformation.

It was the fire of London that provided England with a classical church architecture. Confronted with the opportunity of building fifty new churches in the city of London, Christopher Wren set about designing what he considered distinctively Protestant church buildings. St. Paul's, his greatest work, does not properly come within this category; Wren was unable to carry out his favourite theme in the design of the cathedral, having to settle for a traditional cruciform plan interpreted in his own classical style. But in the building of his city parish churches he had things pretty much his own way. These parish churches were built as "auditory" churches designed to seat as many people as was conveniently possible within the sound of the preacher's voice. Wren laid it down that the pulpit should be placed no farther distant than sixty feet from the most distant worshipper. In some instances the pulpit was actually placed at the front centre of the nave in front of the altar — a position which is retained to this day in Wesley's City Road Chapel. In practically every instance the chancel was reduced to a mere sanctuary just large enough to accommodate the holy table or altar.

In a letter written to Queen Anne in advanced years, Wren summed up some of his convictions gained from long experience as a church builder:

The Churches, therefore, must be large, but still in our reformed religion, it would seem vain to make a Parish Church larger than that all who are present can both see and hear. The Romanists, indeed, may build larger Churches; it is enough if they hear the murmur of the Mass, and see the elevation of the Host; but ours are to be fitted for Auditories.[3]

The Free churches of the seventeenth and eighteenth centuries made their own significant contribution to the architecture of Protestantism. The Nonconformists, as they were called, had separated themselves from the state-sponsored Church of England because they felt that it had not made a satisfactory recovery of New Testament beliefs and practices. It was natural that in the building of their own houses of worship they should

---

[3] *An Outline of Christianity:* The Story of Our Civilization, ed. by A. S. Peake and R. G. Parson, London, The Waverley Book Company, Ltd., Volume 4, p. 180.

depart from an architecture that had been inspired by principles which they no longer held. The buildings which the Presbyterians, Congregationalists, Baptists and other independents erected at this time were, accordingly, plain and vigorous structures largely devoid of decoration. Justice has been done to the architecture and furnishings of these buildings in A. L. Drummond's *The Architecture of Protestantism* and in Martin G. Briggs' *Puritan Architecture*. Unfortunate is the omission from both books of any reference to the chapel which is probably the loveliest and most remarkable of all — the remote chapel at Cote near Bampton-in-the-Bush in Oxfordshire which was built in the 1660's of Cotswold stone. This building preserves to this day its original layout and furnishings, and provides the student of architecture with an admirable example of a building related to the requirements of Nonconformist worship of the seventeenth century.

The architectural problem confronting congregations of "the people called Methodists" was somewhat unusual. John Wesley himself had never intended that his societies should break from the established Church of England. In his own orders he used the Anglican prayer book, exalted the sacraments of the Church, and showed little patience with his followers who tried to get along without systematic forms of prayer and worship — the very name "Methodist" should dispel the misconception that the early societies were unrestricted in their liturgical forms.

Wesley's chapels, accordingly, were meant to provide services ancillary to those of the Church of England. They were places where people could gather to hear evangelical preaching and sing together in Christian fellowship. Thus supplementing the parish churches, they were free to express in their architecture and furnishings the emphases of Whitefield and the Wesleys.

Once the Church of England had made it clear that it did not intend to recognize this evangelical type of ministry, however, the chapels became the spiritual homes of the Methodists. Then a lack of agreement about worship made itself felt. Many of Wesley's followers adopted an order of service patterned closely upon the Book of Common Prayer, using what were virtually Anglican orders without the authority of the Church of England. Others accepted the informal services of the societies as the norm of Sunday worship.

This dichotomy in Methodist worship practices has persisted down to the present day both in England and in America and has reflected itself in the architecture of Methodism. Methodist places of worship on both sides of the Atlantic vary in design from the simplest types of meeting house to the most elaborate structures designed for worship in the high church tradition.

From this review of the history of Christian architecture, brief and sketchy as it is, it is clear that in recovering the principles governing the faith and practice of the early church the Protestant reformers were led, unwittingly for the most part, to recover also some of the most significant features of the physical environment of early Christian worship. We say "unwittingly" because there was no attempt on the part of the reformers to copy an ancient style. At the time of the Reformation the sources of early Christian architecture were little known. The Protestant reformers relied for their insights not so much on literary and visual precedents as on principles of worship that proved to be valid to the experience and needs of the Church in both of those widely-separated periods. Characteristic of the design of both those periods was the simple rectangular building, well-proportioned and uncluttered. The building was shaped as an auditory room so that all the worshippers could see and hear what was transpiring in worship. The pulpit or ambo was given prominence well within the sight and sound of all the people, and the communion table, whether in a shortened apse or well forward in the building, was placed in intimate relationship with the people. The provision in both instances was for a shared ministry of word and sacrament.

So obvious and straightforward were these arrangements that had a worshipper of the third century been able to return at random to the human scene he would probably have felt much more at home in a worship service of the seventeenth century conducted in the setting of the reformed tradition than in a service of the fifth or sixth centuries belonging to the tradition of the as-yet-undivided Catholic Church. What the reformers had done in liturgy and in architecture was simply to bypass the developments of a thousand years and start over again at the point of the New Testament witness.

It would appear, then, that an architecture that would be true to the insights of the reformed tradition is more likely to draw its inspiration from the earliest centuries of the Christian era and from the post-medieval period than from the intervening millennium that marked the development of the Catholic era.

7

Post-Reformation

Architecture

The architecture of the seventeenth and eighteenth centuries gave to Protestantism buildings that served, admirably for the most part, its worship requirements. It is time this fact was recognized. For too long Protestants have been apologetic about their architectural heritage. They have accepted uncritically the charge that the Puritans were without taste and that the buildings of Protestantism were devoid of character. Typical is the statement of Benjamin Jowett, the celebrated Master of Balliol College in Oxford, who, after a tour of some of the cathedrals in England, observed: "It is the great misfortune of Protestantism never to have had an architecture. Hence it is always being dragged back through the medium of art into Romanism."

The first part of Dr. Jowett's statement can successfully be challenged. Protestantism after the Reformation developed an architecture which, as we have seen, was true to its best spiritual insights and adequate to its practical needs. It is not so easy, unfortunately, to challenge the second part of Dr. Jowett's statement. It is a fact that Protestant architecture periodically has tended to divert itself into expressions that are alien to its spirit.

The reason for this is not difficult to find. The requirements of a church edifice are unique in that the building, in addition to providing for the practical needs of a shared ministry of word and sacrament, must meet the subtle aesthetic requirements of worship, and must do so in such a way as not to lead the worshipper astray on a merely emotional excursion. Biblical religion is both revelation and mystery, and while Protestantism emphasizes the revealed rather than the mysterious aspects of the faith it is important that the emotional requirements of the worshipper be satisfied if public worship is to make its appeal to the whole nature of man.

The architecture of Protestantism in its Nonconformist expressions was good architecture for an age that was concerned first of all to recover the *raison d'être* of its worship, but it failed to meet the more subtle and, from an architectural point of view, the more difficult problem of satisfying the worshipper's emotional needs. The failure was entirely understandable in the seventeenth century. The Protestant reformers, aware of the very effective manner in which the arts had been abused by the Roman church to create a thearcic mystery out of the sacrament of the Lord's Supper, reacted negatively to their use in reformed worship. The result was that the artistic forces that should have rallied around the Reformation were dissipated and lost to Protestantism.

If man's aesthetic and emotional needs are not met by a contemporary form he will revert to a familiar one for satisfaction. He will go back to whatever ancient form or symbol has proved capable of satisfying his need. This was what happened in the worship experience of Protestant congregations. When Protestantism in the early nineteenth century sought to enrich its worship it found that it had nothing indigenous to draw upon in the field of the arts and it was forced to copy from the archaic past. The Protestant worshipper found his dormant emotions bestirred by artistic forms which in another day and other circumstances had satisfied them.

In the Anglican Church Laud was avenged. Under the determined leadership of members of the Cambridge "Camden Society" and those who were inspired by it many of the medieval practices that Protestantism had discarded were restored to the Church. Gothic architecture, neglected for two hundred years, was revived. John Ruskin was perhaps the most influential figure connected with this revival of the Gothic, and his influence on church architecture in English-speaking lands was perhaps greater than that of any other individual of the nineteenth century. Ruskin had defined architecture as "the art which so disposes and adorns the edifices raised by man, for whatever uses, that the sight of them may contribute to his mental health, power and pleasure."[1] It is significant that among his seven lamps of architecture there is no lamp of function. The form of a Christian church building is determined not by theological terms of reference or even by the practical physical requirements of the congregation but by the generalized standards of beauty, truth, memory, etc., which appeal to any lover of the beautiful and the true. The distinctive merit of the church building is not its Christian quality but its aesthetic appeal.

Carried away by this romantic conception of a church building architects and builders in the last century enthusiastically embraced the Gothic style. "We are now called upon to prove that Gothic is the only true Christian architecture," stated a pamphlet of the year 1844. The attempt was all too successful. It became apparent that people everywhere love a pretty church. In new construction arty imitations of Gothic buildings — invariably in the "decorated" style! — appeared in every burgeoning suburb of the land.

The Nonconformists, whose liturgical practices (or lack of them) forbade the erection of copied medieval buildings, lavished wealth upon enormous churches and chapels, forgetting that the meeting-house loses its functional significance when it becomes a public assembly hall — a double purpose which many of the Nonconformist buildings actually served. England was at the height of her material power and the Nonconformists themselves were in the vanguard of worldly success. It was inconceivable that the churches and chapels of Protestantism should be deprived of the elegance with which the prosperity and wealth of the times could endow them. Nonconformist church architecture, like everything else, succumbed to the infelicities of the times. Builders and decorators began to clutter things up, and Protestant church buildings lost the dignity and the simplicity that had characterized the better structures of the seventeenth and eighteenth centuries.

---

[1] *The Seven Lamps of Architecture,* London, Cassell and Co., 1909, p. 35.

Figure 6. The City Temple, London, before the blitz.

We are all familiar with the appearance of these overbuilt churches of the last century. Typical of them was the old City Temple in London — a large rectangular galleried structure capable of holding an enormous number of people who might gather for either a sacred or a secular occasion. These buildings have been criticized because they were "pulpit-centred." Actually the trouble with them was not that they were pulpit-centred but that they lacked any focus at all. Galleries swept inward, pillars and arches pointed upward, organ pipes marched across the front, and pews circled to mid-centre. The worshipper found himself suspended somewhere in the midst of all that confusion not quite knowing where to fix his attention. He usually ended up by counting the organ pipes or tracing the stencils around the windows (*Figure 6*).

A reaction against this type of thing was inevitable. What is regretable is that the Nonconformists, in trying to rid themselves of Victorian infelicities, bypassed the soundest principles of their own tradition to copy the mistakes which the Anglicans in England, and to a lesser extent the Lutherans on the Continent, had been making. They too, were persuaded to embrace a style of architecture with which, liturgically and doctrinally, they had very little in common — namely, the revived medieval Gothic.

In America, too, church builders, inspired by the leadership of men like Ferguson, Goodhue and Cram, came after the turn of the century to accept neo-Gothic as virtually the only legitimate expression of Christian church architecture. True, significant contributions to church architecture were being made in other fields, notably in the revival of the Romanesque style and the adaptation of Norman and Flemish forms to twentieth-century needs, and the significance of these works executed under the genius of men like Henry Hobson Richardson was recognized. It was recognized, too, that in certain communities such as the New England states where the link with the past required the adaptation of Colonial or Georgian forms, it would be well to retain the classic style. By and large, however, Cram's point of view, expressed in the elegant statement below, carried the day. Conceiving the function of church architecture as primarily that of creating a religious mood and a spiritual glow this gifted and accomplished artist could quite conscientiously say:

Not in the barren and ugly meeting-house of the Puritans, with its whitewashed walls, three-decker pulpit and box pews, were men most easily lifted out of themselves into spiritual communion with God, — not there did they come most clearly to know the charity and sweetness of Christianity and the exalting solemnity of divine worship, but where they were surrounded by dim shadows of mysterious aisles, where lofty piers of stones softened high overhead into sweeping arches and shadowy vaults, where golden light struck down through storied windows, painted with the benignant faces of saints and angels; where the eye rested at every turn on a painted and carven Bible, manifesting itself through the senses to the imagination; where every wall, every foot of floor, bore its silent memorial to the dead, its thank-offering to God; where was always the faint odour of old incense, the still atmosphere of prayer and praise.[2]

How was it that no Protestant theologian arose to point out to Cram and his followers that in Christian worship, at least in its reformed emphasis, men are not supposed to be "easily lifted out of themselves into spiritual communion with God," but that on the contrary men and women are called to a vital faith relationship which establishes community with their fellows through the action of Jesus Christ in their midst?

So strong a hold and so deep an attraction, however, did this sort of thing have upon Protestant congregations that the appeal of the Gothic style and the neo-medieval plan continued virtually unchallenged down to the middle of the twentieth century. For most Protestant ministers and congregations this plan and style have come to constitute the normative "idea of a church," and most of the churches that have been built in Canada and the United States since the close of the First World War have followed it.

Characteristic is the long and rather narrow nave with a centre aisle leading to a recessed chancel. The addition of transepts at the crossing and a clerestory-side-aisle arrangement is frequently a feature of the larger and costlier buildings. The choir is invariably located in stalls on both sides of the chancel, the pulpit on one side or the other at the front of the chancel, and the altar or communion table at the remote east end of the chancel, as far from the congregation as it can be put.

Apart from minor concessions to denominational usage this plan has served Protestant congregations ubiquitously. Congregations in the Baptist tradition, for example, have come to place the baptistery behind the communion table in place of the sedilia or reredos of other churches. Presby-

---

[2] Quoted by William H. Leach, *Protestant Church Building*, New York, Abingdon-Cokesbury Press, p. 86.

terians have usually insisted on bringing the communion table forward from the east wall far enough to enable the minister to serve from behind the table. Anglicans and some Methodist congregations may choose to leave it altar-fashion against the east wall. With minor modifications this plan could serve even a Roman Catholic congregation. Interestingly enough one of the most magnificent churches of The United Church of Canada, the Metropolitan Church of Toronto, described rightly as a "cathedral-like structure," was designed by a Roman Catholic architect, Mr. J. Gibb Morton, and this design is said to have inspired Morton's preliminary sketch some months later of the proposed St. Joseph's Church, Ottawa, home of the English Oblates in Canada.

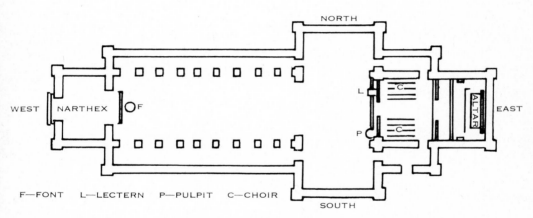

Figure 7. A typical cruciform plan.

Nowhere was the legitimacy of the Gothic style and the neo-medieval plan of a church building more uncritically accepted than in the circle of the Protestant ecclesiologists and worship experts themselves. Most of them jumped enthusiastically and uncritically onto the Cram band-wagon. Note, for example, the theme of T. A. Stafford's book, *Christian Symbolism in the Evangelical Churches,* which offers, presumably as the norm for a congregation in the "evangelical" (sic) tradition a typical cruciform-style structure, complete with deep recessed chancel and railed sanctuary, the whole thing furnished with a welter of medieval symbols (*Figure* 7). "Surely," as

Martin S. Briggs has said, "the Free churches, representing something quite positive and distinctive in their polity and their faith, with three centuries or more of history behind them, should be able to devise a form of architectural expression which should be positive and distinctive, and should not be a mere watering down of obsolete medieval architecture."[3]

The tragedy in the situation is that this conception or this "idea of a church" to which the Protestant has attached his emotions is true neither to the genius of Protestantism nor to the spirit of the twentieth century. It is a double anachronism. In practically every physical and material expression except the design of his churches modern man accepts unquestioningly the impact that twentieth-century techniques have made upon his way of life. The modern businessman demands for himself and his secretary an office that is air-conditioned and bright; the progressive parent insists that the schools which his children attend should be functional and airy; the keen executive scorns having good money wasted on needless bric-à-brac for the new factory; the board of directors is convinced that fake pillars are no longer needed to hold the façade of the new bank. When it comes to building for the glory of God, however, all too many of these very people have remained satisfied with emotional expressions that are sentimental rather than creative, imaginary rather than real.

Architects today recognize the dishonesty in this and the best of them refuse now to have anything at all to do with imitative design in their churches. This refusal is based not so much upon practical as upon moral considerations. While it is true that there are real technical and structural difficulties involved in any attempt to refabricate the past, these difficulties are not half as great as the problem of trying to create a contemporary design that is really adequate to the emotional and spiritual needs of the modern worshipper. The real objection to the continuance of traditional church architecture is moral. The architect and the artist feel today that religion must relate itself to life, and that it is dishonest for the Church to perpetuate institutional forms that belong to an arrested past. "I understand," wrote

[3] *Puritan Architecture,* London, Lutterworth Press, p. 12.

Halverson, "it is one of the axioms of the architectural profession that architecture always tells the truth about the society in which it takes form. However much it may try to disguise itself, its real nature is disclosed because architecture is the most social of all the arts."[4]

The challenge therefore which Protestant church design presents to the architect is the challenge to build so as to retain those insights concerning the function of the Church and the nature of its worship that are lastingly true while providing artistic expression that will do justice to the aesthetic and emotional needs of the twentieth century. Architects and artists recognize that this last need can be met only by a break from tradition. Saint Francis of Assisi is credited with the sobering statement that:

Every fresh movement of the spirit involves casting off of the old body, the old garment. Even the grandest works of art must be treated as reckless trifles, mere improvisations, to be abandoned or destroyed on a moment's notice as soon as they begin to stifle the spirit — abandoned with the faith that while the spirit remains alive it will produce as good or better as soon as needed.

This is the spirit in which Protestantism must face the challenge of its contemporary needs. The argument whether we are in an experimental or creative age in church architecture is beside the point. There can be no creativity without experiment. The fact that much contemporary church architecture — perhaps most of it — is bad does not alter the necessity to keep to the new road. It simply underlines the magnitude of the opportunity that confronts the Church today and the importance of establishing a viable relationship with contemporary architecture and the allied arts.

---

[4] From article in *Architectural Record,* December, 1956, p. 131.

8

A Functional Architecture
for Protestantism

The distinctive achievement of the church architecture of the Protestant Reformation was that it met successfully the requirements of a ministry of word and sacrament that is intimately shared by the whole worshipping congregation. This architecture suffered, however, from a failure to make adequate provision for the emotional needs of the worshippers. The result was that in modern times Protestant architecture was led astray from sound historic principles of design to reliance largely upon aesthetic and artistic devices for the creation of a setting for worship that would more adequately satisfy those emotional needs. Instead of asking "What is the building for?" architects and builders of the late nineteenth and early twentieth centuries found that it was more rewarding to ask "How do the people like it?"

Fortunately for Protestantism the technological revolution that has overtaken construction in recent years has brought the question of function again to the fore in thinking about church design. It is generally recognized that Louis Sullivan's axiom that "form follows function" applies to ecclesiastical as well as to every other kind of design, and that what is needed in Protestant church building today is a design that is architecturally honest and liturgically functional.

It does not follow from this recognition, however, that we have at last arrived at a happy solution of the architectural problem as far as the design of new churches is concerned. Unfortunately it is quite possible for architects and building committees to appreciate the need for a functional design while still entertaining misconceptions and wrong notions concerning the actual function of a Protestant church building. They may be quite honest in their motives and intentions while being misinformed in their concepts.

That this is precisely the case is evident from a glance at the type of Protestant church buildings that have been erected in Canada and in the United States since the Second World War. While it is possible to find buildings the design of which admirably conforms to our definition of the requirements, most of them have been artistically rather than theologically designed. Skilfully planned and beautifully appointed, these churches nevertheless conform more to the sentimental tastes of an affluent society than to the simply-stated needs of a community that is renewing itself in the fellowship of its Lord and Master. The thousands of laminated arches that have been thrust heavenward on this continent in the last ten years for no better purpose than to create a "churchly feel" suggest that the basic misconception of a Protestant church building remains. I am not implying that this particular device should not be used in construction, but I do feel that its almost ubiquitous use suggests that architects and building committees still tend to think of function in terms largely of atmosphere and feeling.

The Reverend Edward S. Frey, executive director of the Department of Church Architecture of the United Lutheran Church of America stated recently at a panel of experts on church architecture:

Designing for form and effect without full concern for substance and liturgical intent is sheer charlatanism. The "atmosphere" which we want our church interiors to have is not achieved by artistic contrivance. What we want is given rather than achieved. It appears in the finished building as a result of having successfully captured in design, insofar as this is possible, the meaning and action of public worship. Because of the liturgical awakening that is occurring in all the churches, the day is almost upon us when nearly any average guy will be able to spot a spurious "religious atmosphere," one that is contrived rather than inspired. An "inspired effect" so far as it can be described by natural terms results from an obvious harmony among the many formal and decorative elements that are proper to liturgical expression.

Refreshing by way of contrast to contemporary American church buildings are the sterner and less compromising Protestant church buildings of continental Europe where structure and furnishings have been reduced to the essence. On studying some of these European churches — and I would not suggest that they are all of merit! — one feels that reasons other than stringent economic necessity underly the critical use of materials in these structures. These churches have made up their minds concerning their distinctive function in the life of the community. They have been built to do precisely what the congregation requires them to do and nothing more.

Obviously there is need for soul-searching on the part of Protestant people in America today concerning the function of public worship and the place of architecture and the allied arts in its service. Timely in this regard is the following statement from an address on "The Church's Responsibility in Worship" delivered by Dean Joseph Sittler to the North American Conference on Faith and Order at Oberlin in 1957:

The human animal is influenced by setting, accompaniments, symbols, silence, the gravity of statement and response, the solidarity-producing impact of solemn music, etc. So it has happened that experts in worship have arisen among us. All assume that the purpose of public worship is to create a mood; and he is the most admirable as the leader of worship who has mastered finesse in the mood-setting devices made available by the application of psychological categories. Thence has flowed that considerable and melancholy river of counsel whereby one may learn how to organize an assault upon the cognitive and critical faculties of the mind, how to anesthetize into easy access the non-verbalized but dependable anxieties that roam about in the solitary and collective unconscious, and how to conduct a brain-washing under the presumed banner of the Holy Ghost.

That this is what worship means in thousands of congregations is certainly true; it is equally true that the Scriptures know nothing about such ideas.

When the function of worship is thus mistakenly conceived as primarily the creation of a religious mood or feeling the arts come to be employed as an end in themselves and the artist, be he architect or symbolist, comes to conceive of his assignment merely as a challenge to his own sense of creativity. He easily comes to mistake self-expression for divine inspiration. Unless he is a convinced and an informed Christian — a rare combination in the field of the arts today! — he is likely to assume that a form which for him is inspired therefore possesses a religious quality that makes it universally valid to public worship.

That latter-day architects are not free from this misconception is illustrated by statements such as those given below which have been taken from recent writings in the field of Protestant Church architecture. Selected more or less at random, these quotations may be said to characterize the general thinking of the architectural profession in this country with regard to the function of a Protestant church edifice. The interesting thing is that the context of all these statements is a conscientious and genuine concern on the part of the profession to achieve excellence in the design of church buildings. The men whose opinions are quoted are men of deep integrity, which makes all the more revealing their misconception of function. One of them who has been eminently "successful" in the field of ecclesiastical design comments:

Here in our town and in the United States we prize above all else individual human growth. . . . The architecture of First Methodist Church of ———— is striving to inspire this concept of growth. . . . Perfection of man, as symbolized by the cross, holds the dominant position within this church. Above it light and clear glass in the sky-window tell us man's possible growth is infinite.[1]

One of the editors of *Churches and Temples* asserts that "Protestantism was founded by simple men with democratic beliefs. It needs an architecture to express it."[2] Another architect, addressing a retreat of The Church Architectural Guild of America, defines the physical church building as

---

[1] Statement by Alden Dow as reported in *Churches and Temples,* New York, Reinhold, 1953, p. 18P.
[2] Op. cit., p. 13P.

"a working tool to aid the layman in his quest of God."[3] Writing on "The Challenge of Church Design" in an issue of the *Journal* of the Royal Architectural Institute of Canada a well-known Canadian architect stated:

The design of a house of worship requires these minimum attitudes: The architect need not be religious, but he cannot be an atheist. He must be able to affirm the creative act. It is unimportant whether he believes God created man in his image or man God in his, for both are creative acts.[4]

It is not being uncharitable to state that from the point of view of sound Christian doctrine remarks such as these serve no better purpose than to illustrate how imperative is the need for a theologically-informed criticism of Protestant church architecture. What must be pointed out to those responsible for the design of churches is that the Protestant worshipper finds the sources of divine revelation neither in the creative impulses of the gifted individual nor in the vague religious aspirations of the worshipper but in the specific content or data of the Christian religion itself which is informed through the sacred Scriptures under the leading of the Holy Spirit. There is no gain to Protestant architecture to substitute for eclecticism the personal tastes and aspirations of a generation of creative individualists.

It is precisely here that the danger of art lies to religion. Art, as Plato perceived, is always tempted to assume an autonomy that may actually be quite at variance with the requirements of the society or the institution that it is commissioned to serve. "An almost overwhelming temptation for all of us, but especially for the architect is the desire to design for emotional effect, art for art's sake, at the expense of liturgical usefulness and significance."[5] The early Christian church, as we have seen, perceived this

---

[3] Article by Arland A. Dirlam "What is the Role of the Architect Designing a Christian Church?" as it appears on p. 7 of mimeographed paper *Questions to Help us Think About Building for Worship,* issued by the Church Building Bureau of the National Council of Churches.

[4] From article "The Challenge of Church Design" by Percival Goodman, A.I.A., *Journal* R.A.I.C., January 1951, p. 14.

[5] From a paper by E. S. Frey, "Public Worship and its Architectural Expression" mimeographed and circulated by the Church Building Bureau of the National Council of Churches.

danger in the arts, and for the first three centuries of its existence refused to have very much to do with them. At the time of the Reformation there was again a vigorous reaction against the arts that resulted in the obliteration of some of the finest cultural achievements of the human race. It was the conviction of many of the Protestant reformers, including men like Calvin who, as we have said, was himself a lover of art, that no art at all was better than an art that substituted its own insights for the truth of the Gospel.

The logic of criticism, however, is not iconoclasm, and the solution of the artistic problem for the Church is not the elimination of the artist but a clear statement from the theologian of the frame of reference within which the artist may be expected to exercise his creativity. Emil Brunner in his book *The Divine Imperative* suggests that art can best fulfil itself when God uses its services "to prepare the way for the Word to enter the soul." The function of art in this context is to intensify the impression made by the word of Scripture and the proclamation of the Gospel. In order to do this well the artist must at least know something of the word of Scripture and the basic content of the Christian Gospel. One would like to believe that our Lord's conditional promise recorded in Saint John's Gospel, "If ye continue in my word . . . ye shall know the truth and the truth shall make you free," can secure for the artist not only sufficient scope for his creativity but a field of operation where he can exercise his gifts most effectively. Historically this has been the case. The finest expressions of architecture, music, sculpture and painting have come out of theological frames of reference. In our day, too, artists and craftsmen should be able to find in the scriptural definition of man's destiny a challenge to their highest creative gifts. Before this can be achieved, however, there will have to be a much closer and much more intelligent dialogue between Christian theology and contemporary culture than has yet taken place in this century.

The securing of good architecture, then, is primarily a theological concern, and if Protestant church architecture in this creative period has failed to rise to its opportunity the responsibility must rest finally not so much with the architects as with the churches whose servants they are supposed to be. For many years now within the Protestant churches, and particularly in churches of the non-liturgical tradition so-called, there has been an almost total neglect of the study of church architecture and the place of the arts in Christian worship. In how many theological schools has this subject even yet been given the significance that it deserves in the field of practical theology? How many ministers are there in Protestant churches possessing anything like a working knowledge of church architecture and liturgical art?

While it would be unreasonable either to expect ministers to be architects or to expect architects to be theologians, it is not unreasonable to expect that a man of the cloth (who will spend most of his professional time in and around church buildings) should at least know some of the elementary terms of church architecture and should be able to communicate intelligently to the building committee and the architect the specific liturgical needs of his people. He should know whether his church is to "have" a sanctuary or to "be" a sanctuary. He should be able to state with conviction just what his denomination and local congregation require in the provision for the sacraments: the size and location of the communion table, the placing of the font, and the relationship of these parts of the furnishings to the action of the congregation. He should be able to define the particular function of the choir in its office of praise and assist the architect to a sensible solution of what too often is an aesthetic and a liturgical botch. He should be versed in the theology of Christian education so that he is clear in his mind as to the relationship between worship and work and instruction as it is actually carried out in the local Sunday and mid-week activities of his people. Lacking such direction the architect should not be blamed if the building turns out to be theologically effete.

Fortunately the Protestant churches are at last awakening to their responsibility in this regard. One of the most hopeful signs of Protestant church life today is the renewed interest in the theological requirements both of public worship and of Christian education. The confluence of Biblical and liturgical studies in recent years has resulted in a re-examination of these requirements, and this in turn has led to a liturgical renewal that is now making its influence felt at the practical levels of church design with regard both to the sanctuary and to the Christian education requirements.

Indications of this are evident from many sides. Particularly interesting and hopeful is the remarkable change that has come over the attitude of some of the denominational boards and bureaus that are charged with leadership and direction in the field. Less than ten years ago Thiry, Bennett and Kamphoefner in their book *Churches and Temples* could reasonably protest against the ineffective leadership of the majority of the bureaus of church architecture in the Protestant denominations of America:

If the bureaus which now provide archaic advice on church design were instead to provide the information which would help an architect to determine the functional requirements of the church, the value of these bureaus would be great.[6]

Anyone who has recently attended a conference on church architecture sponsored by the Department of Church Building of the National Council of Churches and the Church Architectural Guild of America cannot help but be impressed by the manner in which theological considerations are repeatedly being thrust to the fore. Gone are the days when churchmen gathered at these conferences mainly to look at the samples and wares of the "ecclesiologists" — usually representatives of commercial firms that specialize in gold cloth and bleached wood! These conferences invite the participation of theologians of the first rank, who invariably stimulate both architects and clergy to a discussion of principles that are vital to good design.

Perhaps even more significant than the work being done by the denominations are the efforts of interdenominational bodies. The Department of Worship and the Arts of the National Council of Churches and a similar department within the World Council of Churches are attempting to sharpen the focus of the liturgical renewal within the churches so as

---

[6] P. 6P.

to bring its insights to bear upon the practical necessities of church architecture and the related arts.

All this interest and study has helped to create a climate in the field of Protestant church architecture that is wholly conducive to the growth and development of good church design. The minister or layman who now wants to inform himself of sound principles of church design is able to find resources of practical help that were not available a generation ago.

One would like to hope that this architectural renaissance, if we dare call it that, will eventually extend itself through the theological schools of the Protestant churches into congregations where the detailed problems have to be worked out in terms of local needs and opportunities. Through an intelligent appreciation of the possibilities that are now open to architecture and through a critical appraisal of the special needs of the particular congregation it should be possible now to build churches in which the words of the prophet Haggai will find a literal fulfilment: "The glory of this latter house shall be greater than of the former."

9
Aspects of Design

1. A Functional Shape

Undoubtedly the most important single characteristic of a church building is its general appearance or shape. By "shape" I mean the subtle relationship of proportions and parts that gives the building a distinctive churchly appearance. This look or feel, this "churchly appearance," must be interpreted and conceived in terms of the congregation's mid-twentieth-century role. It must be a truly functional shape in the sense that the building fulfils its historic mission to the age in which it lives and makes its witness.

The primary function of a church building must be to serve the needs of a particular community of believers that is inwardly renewing itself in corporate fellowship. This community of believers is no self-indulgent fellowship devoted to its own social, moral and spiritual betterment. It is a community committed to the purposes of God revealed in Jesus Christ. It is called to embody the new order of reality that has come into being through Jesus Christ. Its witness in and to the world derives from the exclusive nature of its calling.

All this may sound truistic but if it is seriously examined it will be seen to have a certain practical bearing upon the physical design and appearance of the building. The architecture of the building ought to declare that the Church belongs primarily to a household of faith which finds its terms of reference outside the social institutions of this world. The building is a failure architecturally if its shape conveys the impression either that the congregation is at ease in its own comfortable fellowship or quite at home in the world. In a day like this the church building should have a disciplined rather than an indulgent look.

We have seen that the early Christian Church was an intensely self-conscious community and that a characteristic feature of the shape of its physical building was that it appeared to be in the world but not of it. Its concern architecturally was to provide for the requirements of its work and witness. The building was not put there to provide "a focus for community life" or to impress the passer-by. Basilican architecture, even in its fullest flowering, showed a quite casual indifference to external effect. Its magnificence was directed within.

Before the end of the first millennium all that had changed, as we have seen, and as the Church began to dominate society its external shape assumed a more imposing form—a form more in keeping with the authoritarian institution that it had become. The Church was now "set on a hill" literally and metaphorically, and it could not be hid. The medieval cathedral was, more than anything else, a proud symbol of the Church's victory over the world.

That dominant motif remains fixed in the imagination of both Roman Catholic and Protestant worshippers and to this day determines, to a greater extent than most people realize, the external shape which they think the church building should take.

It must be admitted, however, that that dominant medieval shape bears no likeness to reality in this mid-twentieth century. Today, as in the earliest days of its life, the Christian Church finds itself in tension with the world. It has again become—and in many parts of the world Christians are aware of the fact—an esoteric fellowship. Even on this North American continent, where it currently enjoys a position of some privilege and prestige, the Church must recognize its subordination to the secular and this-worldly nature of the culture in which it lives (and, in some instances actually prospers). To impress and dominate the community is a function which the Christian Church is no longer able to sustain. As evidence of this fact witness the fate of the uncompleted Cathedral of St. John the Divine in New York City!

To admit the contemporary subordination of the Church to secular culture is not to minimize the importance of the outward appearance of the church building but to recognize the nature of the challenge that confronts the architect and the church builder today. Nikolas Pevsner is credited with the statement that "the function of the church building is to convert visitors into worshippers."[1] A congregation that stands in the evangelical tradition will not want to evade that challenge. In order to meet it successfully, however, the congregation will have to be absolutely honest with itself. Any attempt on the part of the Protestant congregation to create through architecture a status for itself in the community that it cannot sustain is to invite misunderstanding and contempt. Today, as never before, the shape of the church must bespeak its actual function in the world. Dr. Marvin Halverson has stated that

a church building which is effectively designed in terms of the function of the Church and the particular congregation for which the building is erected will have an appropriate form and thus the building may take on the nature of a symbol, saying to the world something of what the church believes.[2]

This is another way of saying that if the architect rightly understands the function of the church edifice and skilfully interprets it the result is bound to look like a church whether or not the shape corresponds to the client's preconceived ideas of what a church should look like.

It is important that this point be made because of the frustration that architects are likely to experience today in church assignments. Preconceived ideas about what a church should look like have such a tenacious hold upon most church building committees that the average architect finds it much easier to give the people what they think they want than to meet the challenge of his assignment creatively.

While it is not within the writer's competence to state how the sense of the Church's mission should be expressed architecturally it is his conviction that the appropriate form or symbol is more likely to be achieved satisfactorily through an honest and functional arrangement of the parts of

---

[1] *Architectural Record,* December 1956, p. 132.
[2] Ibid., p. 131.

the building than through a deliberate symbolic treatment of the architecture itself. The test of the appropriate form is not whether the church building looks like a Christian symbol but whether it does what is required of it in terms of its peculiar work and witness. Let me illustrate: The oval symbol of the fish, *IXΦΓΣ*, is a perfectly good Christian symbol and there are definitely appropriate places for its use in decoration, but to design a church building purposely in the shape of a fish, as has actually been done in the case of the First Presbyterian Church in Stamford, Connecticut, is not necessarily the best way to express the appropriate form (*Figure 8*). The triangle, likewise, is a good Christian symbol and also a good Jewish one, and a church building constructed in the tepee or triangular shape may serve a very practical and useful purpose—as in a snow belt such as Kitimat, B.C., or on the prairies; but it does not follow that church buildings ought now to be constructed, as the late Frank Lloyd Wright suggested, to express "aspiration by triangulation." Invigorating and fresh as some of these shapes (the tepee, the fish, the ship—yes, the circle!) may be, one is led to protest that this is not the best way to make a church look like a church. The way to make a building look like a church is to let it be the church in the most straightforward way possible, relying on the size and shape of the structure, the location of its parts, and the arrangement and relationship of its furnishings to serve the actual needs of the people in terms of their practical requirements for worship, fellowship and instruction. If this assignment is carried out with imagination and skill, the result, I repeat, will look like a church.

As far as the nave is concerned, the plan and the shape that has proved most satisfactory historically has been the simple rectangular building of oblong shape. This kind of structure provides an economic use of space and, if the nave is not too long, a satisfactory arrangement for the seating. If the building is disproportionately long, however, there is likely to be a falling off in congregational participation on the part of the worshippers who sit far back in the nave. If a chancel is imposed on this rectangle with the "sanctuary" placed at the remote east end of the building, the liturgy is likely to lose much of its intimacy. Recognition of this

Figure 8.   First Presbyterian Church, Stamford, Connecticut.

danger has bred dissatisfaction in recent years with the rectangular floor plan, and has led architects and building committees to experiment radically with other shapes and sizes. Churches are being constructed now in every conceivable shape with justification for some of the weirdest designs being found in precedents allegedly set in "the earliest days of the Church's life." Professor Paul Tillich has expressed his preference for a round church, "the people seeing one another."[3] Tillich comments that a combination of pulpit and altar in the centre (presumably the front centre) "would be the ideal solution for now." What Tillich wants, apparently, is the central church with altar and pulpit close to the people. This provision which,

[3]Quoted from Round Table Report given in *Architectural Forum,* December 1955, p. 136.

liturgically, has a very great deal to commend it, can be secured not only through a round church but in various other ways—notably through a Greek-cross-shaped building whose arms of equal length provide seating for all the people—including the choir—around the central altar. This arrangement has found favour in a number of newer churches, particularly those in the Episcopal tradition, and there are interesting developments in this direction. The Episcopal Church of the Holy Spirit at West Palm Beach, Florida, admirably illustrates this kind of design *(Figure 9)*.

While one can appreciate the liturgical motive behind the planning of an altar-centred church one is led to ask whether the practical difficulties of this design do not outweigh the practical advantages. Granted that it is desirable to establish a close relationship between minister and people, it remains to be asked whether this can best be secured by having the people seated in such a way that they are conspicuous to each other. A rectangular floor plan, the nave provided with a sloping floor if need be, can give a congregation the intimacy that is needed for liturgical worship without the disadvantage of having people seated vis-à-vis each other as in a central plan. Moreover, the practical advantage of a plan that provides access to and egress from the nave at one central place is of very great importance. One of the difficulties of a circular or a cruciform plan such as that illustrated is the problem of getting the people to and from the various seating locations in the nave. A rectangular floor plan that provides wide centre and side aisles leading directly to a spacious narthex at the west end has a controlling effect on the traffic and a unifying effect on the congregation. The people know where they are to go and how they are to get there. The psychological advantage of this is very great.

The thing to secure, whatever the plan of the nave may be, is an intimacy which is basically an intimacy between the people and the liturgy and not just between the people and the people. What we do not want to recover in modern Protestant architecture is the type of auditorium where people feel so much at home with each other that the commencement of the service of worship proper seems like an interruption of the human fellowship.

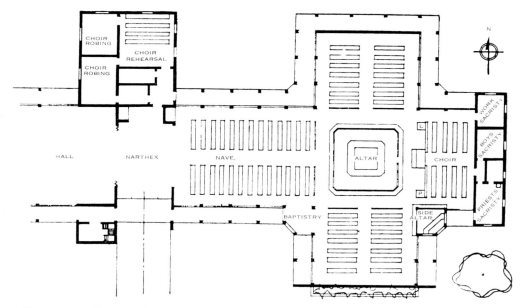

Figure 9.   Episcopal Church of the Holy Spirit, West Palm Beach, Florida.
(Architects: Emily and Harold Obst, Palm Beach.)

Obviously a feeling of intimacy between people and liturgy is easier to secure in a small building than in a large one, and it is a happy circumstance that the modern church has been forced for economic reasons to build churches that are of realistic size in terms of the normal worship requirements of the congregation. Churches today are not being built for the Easter morning congregation. The Department of Church Building of the National Council of Churches states that few Protestant churches are being built in America today with seating accommodation for more than three hundred worshippers:

Sanctuaries are planned on the basis of holding at least 2 worship services, and sometimes 3 regularly, and, on allowing for an average attendance of 50%, with adjustment for local conditions. A seating of 200 plus 25 in the choir, or a total of 225 would accommodate 450 persons in two services (attendance tends to equalize!), and serve a membership of 900 on the basis of 50% average attendance.

It is the conviction of the writer that seating of such restricted numbers as those mentioned above seriously limits the usefulness of the nave, and that it is just as serious a mistake to underbuild as to overbuild. It is a fact, however, that even the largest urban congregations are thinking today in terms of seatings of 500 and 600 rather than in the 1000 or 1200 figures of a generation ago.

The feeling of spiritual intimacy need not be lost, however, just because the building is large in size. Architecturally it is quite possible to establish a sense of intimate relationship between the worshipper and the liturgy in a large edifice by means of proportions and contrasts that emphasize significant relationships of the room and render concentration on certain liturgical areas effective. The strategic use of colour and of light, the fenestration of wall areas—these and other devices skilfully employed can create in any church building, regardless of its size, the particular spiritual atmosphere that most adequately serves liturgical necessity.

By way of illustration, it is quite likely that in a large church the communion table will have to be placed a considerable distance from the majority of the worshippers. The strategic placing of this table, however, with due regard to its size and elevation, and with careful attention to the interplay of light and shade upon it and around it, can establish that particular piece in close relationship with the worshippers. This possibility is admirably illustrated by the design of the interior of Christ Methodist Church in New York City, where the treatment of the altar and the mosaic of Christ in the apse above it creates a feeling of intimacy and warmth that many buildings of smaller size have failed to secure.

Regardless of the size of the church edifice there are certain proportions basic to good design that must be respected if the building is to secure harmony and dignity. S. Giedion, in his stimulating and controversial book *Architecture, You and Me*, has stated:

The whole development of architecture today leads us toward a greater attention to the long neglected study of proportions. We know of course that a knowledge of proportions alone can no more produce a good architect than the rules of sonnet writing can produce a poet such as

Petrarch; but in a period like our own, which is slowly beginning to demand a coherence of parts in relation to the whole, whether in a single building or in a larger complex, the study of proportions can provide a necessary background.[4]

Elementary as this fact is, it would appear that it must be underlined anew for our own day and age. In too many churches that have been constructed in recent years height has been sacrificed for utility, and basic relationships of length and width have not been respected. Clever architectural and artistic devices such as the thrust of a laminated arch from a low wall and the provision of a shaft of light in the ceiling of the chancel have been used to cover a basic indignity in the shape of the building.

Contributing to the bastard proportions of many of our newer churches is the fact that most congregations find it necessary to construct their churches in units or stages. Frequently a small church is built that can later be enlarged by lengthening it or widening it; perhaps the first unit only of a larger scheme is erected. This procedure is all right if the first phase of construction is an integral part of an overall plan that is likely to materialize within a reasonably short space of time. In all too many instances, however, the original plan is not followed through. Frequently the first unit is left to serve purposes for which it was never intended, and additions and extensions are made to it that are anything but harmonious. Nothing spoils Giedion's "coherence of parts in relation to the whole" as effectively as this kind of unrelated construction.

The materials out of which a church is built have a tremendous effect upon the atmosphere of the place, and exert subtle but powerful influences upon the worshippers. Neutra, one of the great contemporary architects, writes: "When we walk through the nave of a medieval cathedral, the impact of our steps on the stone pavement, or the reverberation of a little cough, makes possible, or even becomes, in itself, a vital, essential impression of architectural space." Some materials such as wood panelling are heat gatherers, and induce a feeling of benevolence and warmth. Others

---

[4] Harvard University Press, p. 118.

such as stone conduct heat speedily away and produce a feeling of dignity and grandeur.

The proper use of materials must, therefore, be determined in the light of the structure's basic functions. This subject is too involved and too complicated to enter upon here, and it is certainly beyond the competence of the writer, but its importance is obvious. The question, "What kind of worship goes on here?" must be answered before the question "What is it to be built of?" is considered. Theological necessity must determine technique. It is not up to a lumber salesman to assert that plywood veneer can adequately substitute for solid panelling at the east end, nor is it within the province of a contractor to determine whether terrazzo shall be used instead of travertine in the chancel floor.

In the end of the day theological considerations determine these things and it is better to have them all worked out early in the day than to try to correct them at the end. True, the theologian himself may know little or nothing of the principles of architecture and the techniques of construction. The likelihood, indeed, is that he will be unable to specify in any very helpful way the architectural implications of his own theological views, but what he says concerning the liturgical requirements of public worship and the theological needs of Christian education is bound to have far-reaching effects upon the design of the church building and even upon such commonplace decisions as the use of putty and plaster, stone and wood.

The congregation that aspires to a shapely church must, therefore, inform itself thoroughly of the nature of its worship and its work and then select an architect who is qualified to translate its needs into physical reality. Given a free hand within the terms of reference that have been clearly defined the result, I repeat, is bound to "look like a church."

10
Aspects of Design

2. Functional Parts

The function of a Protestant church building, as we have repeatedly emphasized, is that of fulfilling the requirements in worship and Christian fellowship of a group of people that finds its spiritual identity around the table of the Lord under the preaching of the word of God. Recognition of this fact has come increasingly to the fore in contemporary thought concerning the life and work of the Church. The recovery of Biblical theology in both Protestant and Catholic circles in recent years has been much more than an academic exercise. It has been a realistic expression of the source of the Church's life and strength. In the devastating experiences that have befallen the Christian Church in many parts of the world in recent years congregations have again discovered that it is by the word of God that the Church lives. Coupled with this realization there has been a renewed appreciation of the significance of the Lord's Supper as the expression of the Church's renewal in the body of Christ its Head.

The practical effect of this theological revival and liturgical renewal upon church design has been to emphasize the central importance of both word and sacrament to public worship, and the importance in consequence of the proper placing of both the pulpit and the communion table or altar in the plan of the church building.

There is a real sense in which this liturgical revival finds common ground in both Catholic and Protestant circles. The liturgical movement, so-called, in the Roman Catholic Church today is trying to redress the balance that emphasized the objective sacrifice of the Mass as the action of the priest at the expense of the concept of communion as the action of the entire worshipping congregation. "Build the Church around the altar!" is the instruction now given to architects in Roman Catholic assignments, and some of the most significant work in contemporary church designs is now coming out of Roman Catholic countries. One thinks, for example, of some of the splendid churches that are being built in Latin American countries today, more especially in Brazil which one usually considers a rather backward country theologically.

Just how representative of the thinking of the Roman church this liturgical development actually is remains to be seen, but the manner in which it finds expression in contemporary church design suggests that it represents a significant trend of thought.

Surely Protestant architecture for its part ought to provide a relationship between minister and people that is no less intimate and real than that which Catholicism is seeking to recover. As one looks at contemporary church construction one cannot avoid the conclusion that Catholic architecture is tending to go beyond the logic of its theological position whereas Protestant architecture has not yet caught up with it.

The logic of the Protestant theological position as far as its effect on the arrangement of church furnishings is concerned is to demand freedom of movement on the part of both clergy and people. Edward Sovik, an architect in the Lutheran tradition who is something of a liturgical authority himself, recently had this to say in a letter addressed to a pastor who was concerned with a building programme:

In general, however, I might say that we think we should dispense altogether with the idea of separate nave and chancel so that the activity of worship is dispersed through the space and there is not any dominating focus in the room, but a series of foci—the prayer desk, the pulpit, the choir, the font, the communion table, and other symbols. The design should be such that the congregation is caught in the matrix of the liturgy and cannot easily think of themselves as merely an audience. This is the priesthood of all believers.

It appears to the writer that it is along such general lines as those suggested by Sovik rather than under preconceived ideas of rigid location that Protestant building committees should work out the arrangements of the "sanctuary," by which word we mean, of course, the entire area of congregational worship.

THE PULPIT

Before discussing the location of the pulpit it might be well to define the term. Properly speaking the word "pulpit" or "pulpitum" means that platform on which the minister stands and on which is placed the lectern or lecterns from which the Scriptures are read and the sermon preached. In these pages, however, we shall use the noun in its more commonly accepted sense as the piece of church furniture from which the minister customarily preaches the sermon.

In recent years there has been a tendency to minimize the importance of the pulpit in Protestant church design and to shift it to one side or the other of a divided chancel, its location being determined by such practical and utilitarian considerations as its proximity to the vestry, the acoustic requirements of the building, the general appearance of the chancel, et cetera. The argument frequently advanced for the removal of the pulpit to a lateral position is that it renders the minister less conspicuous and thus lifts the service above the personal plane. Just why the service should be lifted above the personal plane is not usually made clear, and one is tempted at times facetiously to ask the experts in ecclesiology whether there is anything more spiritual about an illuminated dossal curtain than an illuminated individual.

Actually there is sound precedent for retaining the pulpit on the central axis of the building if the congregation so desires. The likelihood, as we mentioned earlier in the text, is that in the fourth century the bishop or president presided from an ambo or desk which was placed at the front centre of the apse. On historical grounds, therefore, no congregation has to feel ashamed of having its pulpit at the front centre of the building. Certainly property committees should very carefully consider the wisdom of converting a building that was designed originally for a central pulpit ministry into something that is radically different. The performance of that operation which we might call the "chancelectomy" has mutilated many a fine old church in this land.

It is interesting to note that in parts of Europe where the reformed and Lutheran tradition is strongest, notably in Holland and in Denmark, many of the newer churches are not only retaining the pulpit on the central axis at the front of the church but are actually emphasizing its centrality by means of huge baffles and canopies and other devices. In these churches there is to be seen immediately in front of the pulpit the communion table, usually very large, free-standing and accessible to all. Commenting on these newer Dutch churches Martin E. Marty recently stated: "The greatest help these churches-for-preaching can provide is this: they have, with pulpit and table at axis, *made up their minds*."[1] (italics mine.)

My plea is not for the central pulpit, however, and it should not be assumed from what has been stated above that the location of the pulpit at the side of the chancel or off-centre in the church necessarily minimizes the preacher's office. Actually if the lateral pulpit is properly scaled and given the elevation that it deserves it can accentuate the importance of the spoken and the preached word (*Figure 10*). Was it not Harry Emerson Fosdick who remarked that the fact that he had to walk over to the great pulpit at the Riverside Church and mount its steps somehow underlined the urgency and the importance of his pulpit ministry! In contemporary church architecture attention is being given not so much to exact mathematical balance as to significance of parts, and where a skilful relationship has been worked out in the arrangement of furnishings the lateral placing of the pulpit may be entirely satisfactory on both aesthetic and liturgical grounds.

THE LECTERN

The writer feels that further thought needs to be given in Protestantism to the precise function of the lectern—a piece of furniture that has

---

[1] *The Christian Century,* February 15, 1959, p. 199.

Figure 10. The City Temple, London, rebuilt.

become almost ubiquitous in newer churches. Does the lectern somehow compromise the "indissoluble unity of word and sacrament"? In the reformed tradition do the reading of the Scriptures and the saying of the prayers require a separate stand? There are indeed practical advantages to providing a place other than the pulpit for some of the acts of the clergy, but one wonders whether the best solution would not be either freer use of the communion table itself or the provision of a twin ambone such as the early church is said to have provided. An ingenious arrangement that has found favour in a number of newer churches is the provision of a secondary desk built into an extension of the pulpit—a kind of throw-back to the days of the double-decker pulpit of Georgian times. In this way the pulpit retains its prominence as the place for the "monstrance of the Gospel" and provision is made for other acts of worship without having to put a piece of furniture where it clutters the area or mars the unity of word and sacrament. An illustration of this arrangement is found in the Applewood United Church, near Toronto, Ontario, the plan of which is shown elsewhere in this chapter.

THE COMMUNION TABLE

Surely it goes without saying that the communion table should be prominently placed and easily accessible to both the clergy and the laity. There should be ample space around it for the minister and the elders to preside without any suggestion of crowding. If the location of choir stalls in the chancel is going to confine the table and seriously restrict movement around it then the stalls should be put elsewhere.

The exact location of the table and even its style and design will depend to a certain extent upon the liturgical practices of each particular congregation. G. W. Addleshaw has remarked that in the course of its history the Christian Church has evolved three different types of altar— the mysterious, the dramatic and the ministerial.

The "mysterious" altar belongs largely to the Eastern Church. Concealed behind veils and iconostasis, it corresponds to the ancient Holy of

Holies of the Tabernacle which was hidden from mortal eyes. The Western Church has never concealed its altar from the laity in this mysterious fashion. The closest that it has come to doing this has been to put it behind an elaborate chancel screen or to place it under a high ciborium.

The "dramatic" altar is of more recent lineage. In the seventeenth century Archbishop Laud succeeded in removing the holy table from the crossing of the medieval churches in England where Protestant practices had put it, and restoring it to the far east end of the chancel. The nine-teenth-century ritualists, inspired by the Cambridge Camden Society, went a step further and, employing dramatic hangings, curtains and reredoses, succeeded in converting the simple table into a dramatic altar.

The "ministerial" altar, so-called because it is literally the place of ministering, is the altar or table accessible to the people, the visible reminder that our Lord perpetuates his own ministry in and through those acts whereby he calls his faithful followers around him and nourishes them with the bread of life. Canon Addleshaw suggests that it is this last kind of altar—the ministerial altar—that best serves the present-day requirements of Anglican worship, and he appears to regard as a retrograde step the gradual transformation during the last century of the ministerial altar into a dramatic worship centre.

It is difficult to avoid the conclusion that an altar fixed rigidly against the east wall is incongruous with the Reformed tradition. Dr. Henry Sloane Coffin's advice is timely:

The table should be unmistakably a table, recalling the table in the Upper Room about which Christ's followers gather, and where he, spiri-tually present, meets them. It should not be set against the wall, for in the Primitive Church and in the Reformed tradition the minister stands behind it, facing the congregation, in order that his symbolic acts may be seen.[2]

It is the writer's conviction that the best place for the table, even from an aesthetic point of view, is well forward from the east wall. If the table

---

[2] *The Public Worship of God,* Westminster Press, 1946, p. 59.

is flush against the wall no vista remains subtly to beckon the mind's eye to the higher fulfilment of its spiritual vision. A feeling of "beyondness" will actually help the worshipper to relate himself to the action of the liturgy whereas a worship centre fixed against the wall, be it ever so elaborate, will suggest that the worship has exhausted itself in the celebration of the liturgy. Is it not desirable that the environment of worship should convey something of that *mysterium tremenduum* that transcends human ingenuity and reason? This can be conveyed better through understatement than through costly and elaborate striving for effect. Stated Paul Tillich: "I do not hesitate to say that I am most satisfied by church interiors—if built today—in which holy emptiness is architecturally expressed; that is of course quite different from an empty church."[3]

This subtle feeling of mystery or transcendence can be effectively destroyed, however, if, after placing the communion table where it ought to be one clutters up the area around it or behind it with furnishings and decorations. Nowhere is Ruskin's rule of restraint better applied than in the furnishing of the chancel. The seat for the clergy behind the communion table should be inconspicuous. Elaborate sedilias, reredoses and other devices that contribute nothing to the communication of the Gospel should be excluded. East-end windows are of very doubtful value. Usually they provide a glare and invariably they call attention to their good or bad taste. Dossal hangings should be used with restraint. Anything that smacks of the theatrical or of the merely decorative must be assiduously avoided.

THE CROSS

Particular care should be paid to the use of the cross. In too many of the newer churches the cross has become something of a cliché. From the Nonconformist churches' almost total neglect of this sacred symbol the pendulum has now swung to crass artistic abuse. In too many instances today architects are using the cross merely as an artistic device—in some instances, one feels, as an artistic device to compensate for their own failure

---

[3] *Architectural Forum,* December, 1955.

to design a church that looks like a church in its own right. Under no circumstances should this most sacred symbol of the Christian faith be used merely as a decorative feature of the building.

THE BAPTISMAL FONT

An important place should be made in Protestantism's shared ministry for the sacrament of baptism. The sacrament of baptism is, among other things, the act whereby a person is first recognized as a member of the Christian community and "engaged to be the Lord's." It is fitting, therefore, that the sacrament should be administered in the presence of the entire congregation and that the font itself should be an integral part of the furnishings—not something put in as an afterthought, as too often appears to be the case. Baptism without public witness is alien to every right instinct of the Christian tradition.

In the majority of the liturgical churches so-called, the font is placed close to the main entrance at the west or back end of the building where its location serves as a visible reminder of the initiatory aspect of the sacrament of baptism. The reasons for putting the font at the back of the church are historical and good. One feels, however, that in the reformed tradition this sacrament should bear a positive relationship to the ministry of the word of God. What is said and done in baptism is rooted in the reality of the revelation that has been given in the sacred Scriptures. It would seem desirable, therefore, that churches adhering to the reformed tradition should place the font where the congregation can witness and share the sacrament in relation to other acts of public worship.

The solution of the problem would appear to be the placing of the font close to an entrance at the front of the building where, together with pulpit and communion table, it serves as a visible reminder of the unity of the church's ministry of word and sacrament. In Calvin's *Draft Ecclesiastical Ordinances* it was laid down that "the stone or baptismal font is to be near the pulpit."

THE CHOIR

The answer to the question of where the choir should be seated and the organ located will have to be given by the architect, the musician and the liturgist together. The architect's task is to reconcile to his own standards of good taste and utility the sometimes-conflicting demands of the musician and the liturgist. The musician will want the choir and the organ put where they will sound best. The theologian will insist that they go where they can best serve the liturgical requirements of a service of public worship. The architect will try to satisfy these requirements in such a way that the building will look aesthetically right. The problem has been stated very succinctly by Addleshaw and Etchells in the paragraph below:

The problem, therefore, which as long as there are choirs in the present sense of the word will always be difficult and complex, is to find a place for the singers from where they can give a due contribution of dignity to the service and also appear in a real relationship to the congregation, leading them in the worship rather than seeming apart from them, and at the same time not dividing the people from the altar.[4]

Practically all Roman Catholic churches and most Lutheran churches have adopted the location in the west balcony over the narthex or vestibule as the most satisfactory place for the organ and the choir. An increasing number of churches in the non-liturgical tradition are coming to accept this location as well. This west balcony position has certain real advantages. An organ sounds to advantage if it is placed high in the building. In the back gallery the choir can be grouped unobtrusively around the organist and the leader. The chief disadvantage of this location is that the choir is isolated both physically and psychologically from the rest of the worshipping congregation. The choir may come to feel that it is on its own back up there. Another disadvantage, if it is a disadvantage, is that there is no point in having a processional if the choir is in such a location.

Actually the chancel and the rear-gallery locations are by no means the only alternatives to the front choir-loft arrangement now generally in disrepute. An interesting arrangement was proposed some time ago by

---

[4] *The Architectural Setting of Anglican Worship,* p. 236.

Edward M. West in an article entitled "Liturgy and Architecture in the Service of Vital Religion" which appeared in *Current Religious Thought* in its March, 1950, issue:

It is wise to consider placing the choir behind the altar and on the same level as the congregation. This still permits the ceremonial use of a vested choir, but more important, it makes the choir itself a portion of the worshipping congregation. The organ console may then be sunk in the floor behind the altar. This leaves the strongly-lighted altar, on its three steps, as a psychological curtain between the singers and the congregation—the most effective screen yet devised. It gives the organist control of his choir and enables him to hear the complete mixture of sound as it will reach the congregation. By keeping the chancel recess sufficiently shallow, the choir will be able to see the preacher, which is most desirable. To hear a voice and see no man was found to be disconcerting even in apostolic times.

Interesting variations of the chancel plan are being worked out in some of the newer churches. A sensible solution is to make the chancel the full width of the nave, thus providing space for full choir on one side or the other of the chancel. The space opposite may be reserved for elders or members of the junior choir. Another possibility is to employ an asymmetrical design with an off-centre aisle and communion table which makes possible the placing of the choir on one side of the chancel with the pulpit opposite on the other. In either of these arrangements the choir can be grouped together as a single unit in full view of the organist, and the minister can be seen by the members of the choir. The whole effect, if skilfully worked out, can be one of satisfying imbalance.

Many interesting possibilities open up if a congregation can rid itself of the medieval obsession that a chancel has to be recessed or indeed that a church has to have a chancel at all. The fact is that in the tradition of the Protestant and the reformed churches there are perfectly good reasons why the chancel should *not* be recessed and the likelihood is that the church of the future will see less and less of concealed organ chambers and divided choirs. Things will be put unashamedly out in the open where they ought to be, and the relationship of the parts will be more intimate and real than has been the case in the recent past.

Figures 11-14 are sketches of locations for the choir that may be adapted to buildings large or small. In each of these we have a compactly grouped choir that should be able to give effective leadership while participating fully in corporate worship.

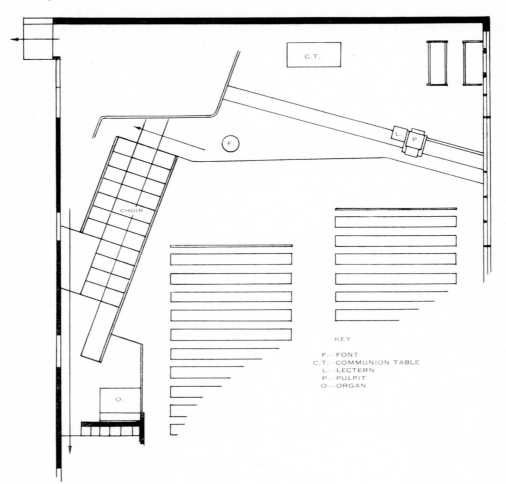

KEY

F.—FONT
C.T.—COMMUNION TABLE
L.—LECTERN
P.—PULPIT
O.—ORGAN

Figure 11. Applewood United Church, Port Credit, Ont.
(Architect: James A. Murray, Toronto.)

The pulpit and lectern are combined to the right of the communion table. A valid criticism of the choir layout is that the choir faces away from the communion table.

This new approach will prove particularly beneficial with regard to the placing of the pipe organ in the building. Happily the day is passing when the worshipper has to focus his attention upon an array of gilded organ pipes. There is no need, however, to go to the other extreme and pretend that the pipes are not there at all. Simple unpainted pipes at the side of the nave or in a transept are not objectionable and they are more honest than costly and elaborate screens that deceive no one and serve no better purpose than partially to muffle the sound of the instrument.

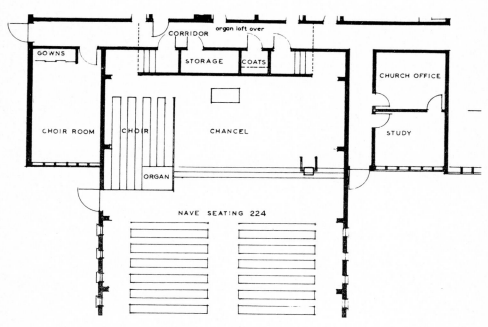

Figure 12. Westridge United Church, North Burnaby, B.C.
(Architect: William Wilding, Vancouver, B.C.)

The liturgical centre of this church is simply a part of the nave. The communion table, however, should be brought forward closer to the nave seating.

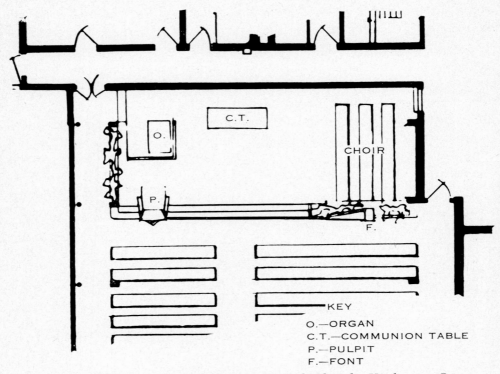

Figure 13. Chancel of St. James' United Church, Kitchener, Ont.
(*Architect: John Lingwood*)

Note in this design how imbalance of plan makes possible a full choir on one side of the chancel.
Centre aisle leads directly to communion table, both of which are off centre.

Organ builders naturally advise having the instrument placed in the location where it will sound best. It is a well-known fact that the higher the organ is placed in the building and the more open the space around it the better it will sound. The American Guild of Organists comments:

In countless instances a beautiful organ has been tonally smothered and reduced to marginal effectiveness by placing it in inadequate and poorly designed "chambers." This burial of the organ developed in the romantic era and has conspired with heavy and ornate grills and cases to waste millions of dollars. Unhappily this practice still continues. *It is the considered opinion of the Committee that a $25,000 organ in a proper acoustical and* *spatial environment will be more musically effective than a $50,000 instrument suffering under the handicap indicated above.*[5]

Everything depends, of course, on what is expected of the choir and the organ in the way of musical effect, and a great deal depends, too, on the size of the building. It is quite likely, however, that the church of the future will think less of the size of its instrument and more of its capabilities in terms of congregational accompaniment. In most churches in this coun-

[5] *Good Acoustics in Churches,* a book prepared in mimeographed form by a special committee from The American Guild of Organists, The Associated Organ Builders of America and The American Institute of Architects, n.d., p. 5.

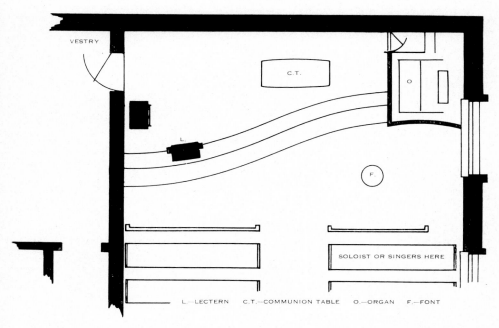

Figure 14. Chapel of Lundy's Lane United Church, Niagara Falls, Ont.

(Architects: Parrott, Tambling and Witmer, Toronto.)

The curvature of the steps leading up to the communion table leaves ample room for baptismal font and also space for soloist or singers who stand adjacent to the organ. The screen at the front of the pews on the right side is broken so that soloist or singers may be seated in front pew. (See p. 115)

try the organs have been too large and too costly for the buildings they adorn. Too frequently the instrument has been designed from the recitalist's point of view rather than as an accompanying instrument. In seeking brilliance for special effects churches have lost much of the charm and beauty of the old low wind-pressure instruments. In this regard it is gratifying to see the recovery by an increasing number of organ builders on this continent of classical specifications for their instruments. They are now getting away from the heavy diapason sounds and the preponderance of eight- and sixteen-foot pipes and are concentrating on instruments with pipes of higher pitch that give brilliance of tone and, consequently, better leadership to congregational singing.

The fact is that the renaissance evident in church architecture has extended itself to all the liturgical arts including those devoted to the praises of God. It is interesting in this connection to recall the plea that was made in 1951 in a report of the Archbishops' Committee of the Church of England in a statement entitled "Music in the Church." Urging that the arts and above all music should be pressed into the service of the Church because "they give form to the Church's sense of the glory of God, the Numinous and the Sublime," the statement added that the supreme test to be applied to the use of the arts in worship is the measure in which they actually serve the liturgical purposes of the congregation in the public worship of God.

Is the motive that inspires their use the Glory of God? Or are they designed rather to attract a congregation? It is peculiarly necessary to keep this test in mind where music is concerned, because music is the most intimate, and in some ways the most subtle of the arts. A practical application of the test is to inquire whether the music is worthy to be wedded to the noble language of the liturgy, which must neither be demeaned nor overwhelmed by musical adornment. The music of the Church is primarily liturgical music.

It is gratifying to realize that developments in the field of church music and organ building in the last decade have been clearly in the direction of a recovery of those standards of excellence for which pleas such as that above have been made.

11
Aspects of Design

3. Related Areas

The neglect in these pages thus far of any serious consideration of the educational, social and recreational requirements of a local congregation in its building needs does not imply an indifference on the part of the writer to the importance and necessity of these requirements in the total picture of the Church's life and work. The fact is that the effective proclamation of the Gospel in this day and age calls for an educational and social programme that makes a major claim upon the Church's resources.

The reason I have confined my comments mainly to the provisions that have to be made for corporate worship is that corporate worship itself sums up the basic nature and meaning of the Church. Corporate worship is the act that sets forth most realistically the relationship of members to the body of Christ. The pattern for all parish activities is the "life in Christ" which is made possible only to a community of faith.

It is recognition of this fact that has led Protestant churches in recent years to rethink their educational and social tasks and to attempt to secure sound theological bases for all phases of the Church's work and witness. Theodore Wedel once remarked that "a Woman's Guild does not automatically become a hotbed of Christian charity by meeting in a church parlour."[1] No social activity of congregational life should ever be

---

[1]Quoted from article "The Lost Authority of the Bible" in *Theology Today,* July, 1952, p. 166.

thought of as an end in itself. The only justification for the multiform activities that occupy an ever-increasing part of the congregation's time in the average Protestant church today is that they are helping to build up the body of Christ in Christian knowledge, in Christian fellowship and in Christian service. Whether this is actually the end that some of these activities serve is a moot point, but that it is the only conceivable justification for what goes on inside any part of a church building is not open to question. The ancillary services of the Church, so-called, are ancillary to only one thing — the knowledge and love and service of the God who has revealed himself in Jesus Christ to a community of faith.

It is important that the architecture of the church building, in all its parts, should demonstrate this fact. The general appearance of the structure and the layout of its parts should be such that the community perceives that it is a church that stands in its midst and not something else. The Reverend J. Gordon Chamberlin, minister in charge of Christian Education at the Riverside Church, New York City, has stated:

If architecture is to express both the theological nature and the practical situation in Protestantism, then the educational facilities must be as clearly and explicitly "the church" as the nave. There are particular difficulties in this for the architect, because most Protestant churches being built in America today require much more square-footage for education than for worship, fellowship or administration. This means that the architectural expression of the education facilities will and should influence the form and character of the whole building.[2]

There are practical ways of effecting this integration. The availability of land in newer developments makes possible a harmonious relationship of the various parts or units of the church building. The higher rise of the nave or the soar of a campanile or tower can draw to itself the adjacent wings and annexes in such a way as to emphasize the unity of the parts that make up the entire church structure. The use of a central courtyard around which the educational and social areas are built offers interesting possibilities to design; it also raises a subtle theological problem. Modern

[2] "Religious Education and the Design of Protestant Churches", reprinted from *Architectural Record,* December, 1959.

methods of construction employing a generous use of steel and glass now make it possible even in these northern climes for architecture to relate itself successfully to its natural environment. In contemporary church buildings earth and sky and walls and floors can now interpenetrate. Just because the possibilities here are so rewarding the church should exercise a certain critical judgment in its use of glass. There are areas and places in the Christian education building such as corridors and stairwells, offices, and church parlours where bright vistas and open prospects are desirable. There are other areas and places where the church should shut itself off from the world of nature. Chamberlin, whom we quoted above, raises an objection to "light and openness" on the level of theological criticism:

Contemporary architecture has freed the church from cramping limitations of trying to adapt old styles to new functions, but contemporary patterns have smuggled in their own inherent symbolism. One of these is the use of light, of glass, of openness, of freedom. Light and openness can imply that all that Christianity means is obvious, only to be seen to be understood. No mystery, distance, judgment, and demand are left. Yet darkness has positive meanings for which light cannot be substituted. The church is not all "light."

Those of us who have been exposed to Christian education facilities as they exist or fail to exist in most churches are not going to put Chamberlin's objection to "light and openness" at the head of the list of criticisms of new buildings. His point, however, is well taken.

It is the writer's conviction that the proper placing of the narthex can do much to satisfy the need for correlation of the parts of the church building. In the past it has been the custom for builders almost invariably to put the narthex at the west end of the nave and to place the entrance to the Christian education facilities off to one side or to the rear of the church proper — an arrangement that very effectively suggests that the educational and social activities of the congregation are unrelated to its worship. From a psychological and theological point of view this is undesirable. There is no good reason why a person who is coming to any part of the church should not be made aware that he is coming to church. He should not have to creep surreptitiously around to a side door because he wants to go to the kitchen or to the gymnasium.

A happier correlation results if the narthex can be related to all the areas of the church building. If it can be located in such a way that it is close to the main traffic areas without itself being used as a general artery so much the better. The solution, where a congregation can afford it, would seem to be the provision of both a narthex and a vestibule, the latter serving as the traffic artery to all parts of the building with the

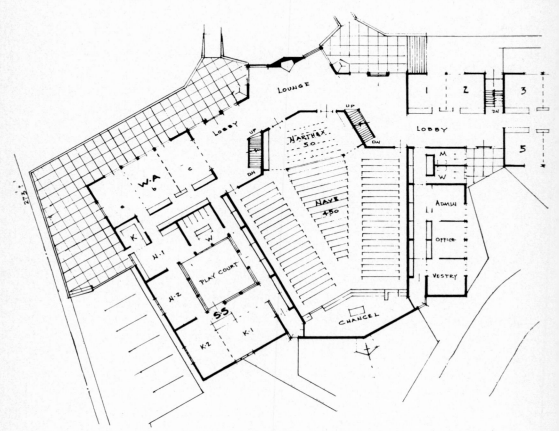

Figure 15. Plan of University Hill United Church, Vancouver, B.C.
(Architect: James E. Dudley)

This plan shows an interesting relationship of parts. Grouped around the main body of the church are units for administration, fellowship, youth work and infants (the latter planned around play court). Spacious corridors relate all these areas. Note the separation of the narthex from the large foyer adjacent.

narthex serving its traditional function as a separated area of the nave. It is desirable if possible to provide architecturally a spatial relationship that enables the worshipper to "take the measure" of the sanctuary before he actually enters it (*Figure 15*). This is not the function of a corridor or a vestibule but it is the function of the narthex.

One of the difficulties facing the church architect is that of estimating the long-range needs of the congregation he serves. From his wide professional experience in general design he should have no difficulty in meeting the ordinary practical requirements of its educational and social programme. He knows much more about kitchen facilities, wash-room locations, corridor regulations and even class-room requirements than the members of the building committee themselves are likely to know. It is more difficult for him to assess the future requirements of a church, however, for its programme is more general in scope and more flexible in operation that that of other institutions, and the congregation is likely to change radically in both its personnel and its interests within a fairly short period of time. What especially affects many churches today is the urban population shift that results in the replacement of Protestants by members of other religious groups or by classes whose habits of church-going have altered from the old pattern. These sociological factors may affect the picture of the congregation's physical needs long before the building itself has become obsolete. Many a congregation in the "inner belt" of great cities is finding today that its gargantuan "plants," considered the last word in efficiency and attractiveness a generation ago, no longer function effectively in terms of modern requirements of Christian fellowship and Christian education.

While it is not possible to predict with any degree of accuracy the long-range needs of a congregation, particularly in an urban area, experience indicates that there are certain functions that remain constant to the Church's work and witness, and provision for these functions is basic.

One of these is certainly administration. Regardless of the changing circumstances that affect the congregation's life and work, the task of administration has to go on. The vestry and office area is the nerve centre of the church and provision should be made at the outset for the kind of administrative set-up that will give the minister and the church staff, whether paid or voluntary, the space and accommodation that they need in order to do their best work. Pastoral interviews and personal counselling are likely to continue to play an important role in the pastoral office and increasingly it is recognized that this work can be done better from the church than from the minister's residence. An attractive room adjacent or close to the administrative area can serve a practical purpose as a consulting room, and when it is not needed for interviews it can be used for other purposes.

The writer's conviction is that all but the smallest churches require a chapel or its equivalent for gatherings of a devotional nature. No congregation will ever find devotional exercises redundant to its needs. It is important that such a room be located where it can easily be reached. It should be close to a main entrance but not adjacent to noisy areas such as the gymnasium or kitchen. If the chapel is in the proper location and if it is suitably furnished it will serve many useful purposes in congregational life. The junior congregation will be able to use it for its worship services. Senior or adult departments of the church school can have their opening devotional exercises there. Evening services may be held there. Small weddings will gravitate to it. Apart from the many practical uses to which it will be put the provision of such a room will serve to "tone up" the entire Christian education building. People who pass its doors will realize that they have come to a building whose activities are meant to be Christ-centred and not oriented simply to human needs (*Figure 16*).

The most important consideration in the design of the Christian education building is to have defined areas which, though flexible enough to serve multiple purposes, prove to be practical for specific categories of age and interest. One of the areas that will have to remain largely specialized is the space for infants and small children. Bright and airy quarters should be reserved for nursery children, toddlers and beginners, and these rooms should be located, if possible, on the ground floor level close to a main entrance. Parents should not be expected to carry infants up and down stairs to their rooms. Facilities for elderly people, too, should be on the ground floor level. A sensible arrangement would seem to be the location of the administrative area and the chapel and the church parlour in a compact unit on the ground floor, with another ground floor unit reserved for infants and small children.

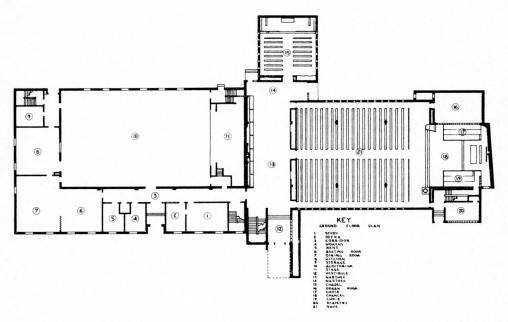

Figure 16. Lakeview United Church, Regina, Sask.
(*Architect: H. K. Black*)

A functional arrangement of related areas.

Noise is the bane of church activities, and just as important as having ample space is the necessity of having functional space — functional, that is, in the sense that the areas can really be usable at those times when it is desirable and practical to use them. The writer knows of one Christian education building, attractive in appearance, beautifully furnished and hailed as "the last word in contemporary design," which has proved anything but functional because of its "open-planning." The rooms are so open and the areas so inviting that every organization hears what is going on everywhere else in the building. With careful planning it should be possible to locate corridors and service areas and class rooms in such a way that they serve as buffers between the main units. By way of illustration: There is no need for noises in the church kitchen to vitiate a programme in the church hall nearby. A Sunday school class room placed between the kitchen and the hall can function very effectively as a serving room during the dinner and be closed off immediately afterwards to serve as a sound barrier while the dishes are being cleaned up and washed. Needless to say a gymnasium or games room should not be on the upper level of a building. Noise, unlike heat, descends, and the place for noise is on the ground where bedrock or the good earth can absorb it.

In the recent past social and recreational halls have frequently been made too large for the practical needs of Christian education and fellowship. While it may be desirable to provide a gymnasium of regulation size for the benefit of a dozen or so young men and women who will play basketball occasionally it may be even more desirable to cut down the size of the room for the convenience and intimacy of the hundred and fifty boys and girls of the intermediate department of the church school who will have to use the hall every Sunday as their place of assembly.

Many things are ideal and desirable that are not quite practical, and one feels sometimes that the Christian education experts in their very admirable concern for the ideal tend to get carried away by their enthusiasm. Illustration of this is provided in the recommendation of the Department of Church Building of the National Council of Churches which lays down among its basic minimum requirements that a church kindergarten serving children of ages four and five should provide thirty-five square feet of floor space per pupil with not more than twenty-five children assigned to each room. Since kindergarten is a specialized age the room or rooms would have to be reserved almost entirely for this one group. In rapidly growing suburban communities where most of the newer church construction is taking place the nursery and kindergarten children are likely to be the most numerous, and in order to fill the basic requirement for a church school having even fifty kindergarten children it would be necessary to provide two very large rooms each of them having at least 775 square feet of floor space — this in addition to the separate washroom, coat room and storage space that is recommended for this department. Obviously the provision of specialized space of this kind that is likely to be used only for a couple of hours during the week lays an unrealistic burden upon the resources of a church that is just trying to establish itself.

Few and far between are the congregations that can afford to meet the needs and desires of every age and interest group of the congregation in terms of the ideal. The best that most congregations can provide is flexible space that is functional within a general range of age and interests. Just because so much is required today in facilities for Christian education and Christian fellowship the design of these facilities, more even perhaps than the design of the sanctuary, lays upon the congregation the responsibility of analyzing with the utmost care the requirements of the various organizations and activities in terms of their specific mission in and to the local church. The congregation owes it to the architect and to the building committee to state in clear and understandable terms precisely what educational and social tasks it is attempting to perform. If it faces this challenge realistically it will find itself involved in theological principles that will be seen to have a very direct bearing upon even the most practical and down-to-earth phases of its life and work.

12

Some Interesting Solutions

In the preceding chapters I have discussed Protestant Church architecture against the background of the historical requirements of worship, with particular attention to the needs of the early Christian church and the churches of the Protestant reformation. I have attempted, further, to relate those requirements to the challenge of an age that is rapidly accustoming itself to new architectural forms. My plea has been that those churches that profess to be informed by the moving and guiding of the Holy Spirit should unhesitatingly embrace contemporary architectural forms, confident that such forms can admirably serve the present-day needs of their worship and fellowship if the churches themselves clearly set forth the terms of reference of their worship and their work.

Bearing in mind the very sensible advice of Alice in Wonderland to the Hatter that "the best way to explain it would be to do it" I shall attempt now to illustrate how what ought to be done is actually being done. In these concluding pages I have selected half a dozen Protestant church buildings, some of them of very recent construction, which to my way of thinking represent successful solutions of particular architectural problems. The difficulty here, of course, is one of selection. Undoubtedly better illustrations could be found. These are submitted because they appear to show recognition of some of the basic problems of design which we have been considering.

No two congregations are quite alike in their physical needs. It should go without saying, therefore, that a building that admirably serves the practical requirements of one congregation may fail utterly to meet the needs of another. It is for this reason, I suppose, that the best of the architects are reluctant to show building committees "pictures" of their work and take them on conducted tours of churches that they have already built. They don't want building committees to form preconceived ideas of what will be attempted. They want each assignment to be a custom job.

It should be understood, therefore, that the illustrations given below are provided not with the thought that what has been done successfully in one situation can be copied in another but rather for the purpose of illustrating the manner in which a number of local congregations have demonstrated in the successful solution of their particular problem the validity of those general principles of design that we have been considering. While it is true that no two buildings will ever serve exactly the same needs, is it not also true that every church building should appear catholic to the extent that it provokes the feeling, "This is the right kind of church for this situation"? If the building elicits that kind of a response it merits the right to be beheld by all even though it should be copied by none.

CHRIST CHURCH, METHODIST

New York City

Architects—Cram and Ferguson, Boston

This building, which was erected in the early thirties at the corner of fashionable Park Avenue and Ninetieth Street in New York City, illustrates the manner in which a congregation has tried to maintain its witness in a crowded city where business and commercial interests dominate the scene (*Figure 17*). The cost of land and services is so high in midtown Manhattan that even the most affluent of congregations can secure little more than toehold space on prominent streets. Aware that the building would be overshadowed by towering apartments and business blocks the architect, Ralph Adams Cram, deliberately forsook his favoured Gothic to build a modern church "in accordance with the principles that controlled what might be called the primitive architecture of the Primitive Church."

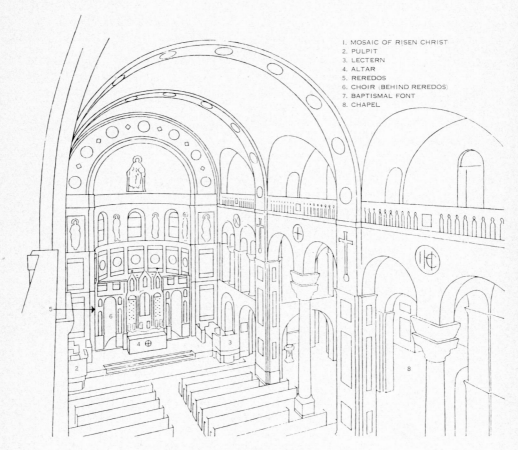

1. MOSAIC OF RISEN CHRIST
2. PULPIT
3. LECTERN
4. ALTAR
5. REREDOS
6. CHOIR (BEHIND REREDOS)
7. BAPTISMAL FONT
8. CHAPEL

Figure 17. Christ Church (Methodist), New York City.

This statement is significant coming from Cram, for Cram, as we have seen, was a devotee of the Gothic. In this particular assignment, however, he saw its irrelevance. "A Gothic Church," he confessed, "should properly dominate its surroundings, which in the heart of a city is impossible. It seemed therefore that this explicitly early Christian style (an adaption of the Byzantine) was one which adapted itself with great delicacy to the requirements." Cram's adoption of the basilican plan and the Byzantine style, carried out with utmost fidelity to detail, was prompted not so much by the desire to revive an ancient form as by recognition of the need for a searching reappraisal of the architectural function of a Protestant church building in the heart of a great city.

Christ Church was built thirty years ago and a fair criticism can be made that the building today appears to be too imitative of a period piece to provide inspiration for the twentieth century. It is the writer's conviction, however, that the plan of this church with the interesting arrangement of its liturgical parts illustrates very admirably the relevance of early Christian architecture to contemporary Protestant needs.

It will be seen from the accompanying plan that the altar is well forward at the front of the apse and that the twin ambones serving as pulpit and lectern are likewise placed in intimate relationship with the worshipping congregation. There is a happy solution to the choir problem. The singers are in the semicircle of the apse in full view of the organist who is seated behind the altar concealed entirely from the congregation by the iconostasis. The side chapel, furnished with chairs rather than with fixed pews, is really an extension of the north side-aisle and provides additional seating to the nave. This flexible arrangement makes possible a church of realistic size in terms of ordinary attendance requirements with provision for larger congregations readily available when needed. Interesting is the relationship of the narthex-vestibule area to the parts of the building. The narthex leads directly both to the nave-chapel and to the educational-administrative area.

The forceful impression that one receives on entering is a feeling of warmth and intimacy that belies the actual size of the building for while Christ Church is not large as New York churches go it is far larger than one realizes. This feeling of warmth and intimacy has been achieved architecturally through careful proportioning of the parts, no expense having been spared to give the building verticality. The intimacy has been achieved artistically through the magnificent mosaic treatment which draws the worshipper's attention to the apse with its spiritualized figure of the living Christ as dominant motif.

Christ Church is one of the most significant Protestant church buildings to have been erected in this century and deserves more attention than it has received in circles of Protestant church architecture.

REGENT'S PARK UNITED CHURCH
St. Vital, Winnipeg, Manitoba
Architect—Norman C. H. Russell, Winnipeg

This building, the interior of which is shown (*Figure 18*), was constructed in St. Vital, Winnipeg, in 1958 for a congregation that had experienced rapid growth. Seating is provided for six hundred worshippers in the nave, and for the choir in the balcony over the narthex. The building is oblong in shape with a flat ceiling and semicircular apse at the front end. Since the architect did not have to make provision for the choir at the front of the church he was able to design the apse entirely with a view to liturgical needs. The communion table is free standing, with ample space around it for the elders who can all be seated in the apse. The pulpit and lectern are well scaled, and the furnishings are in excellent taste.

An interesting feature of the design is that the stairway to the choir balcony rises off the nave rather than off the narthex. Procession to and from the choir loft is thus made through the nave itself rather than through the narthex, a feature that helps to relate the choir to the rest of the worshipping congregation.

The Regent's Park building, although of contemporary design, has a definitely traditional feel, the splendid proportions and the provision of the apse giving it a basilican flavour. Sound principles of design both of the early church and of the reformed tradition have been applied in this instance to the requirements of contemporary Protestant architecture.

Figure 18. Regent's Park United Church, Winnipeg, Man.
"Word and Sacrament"

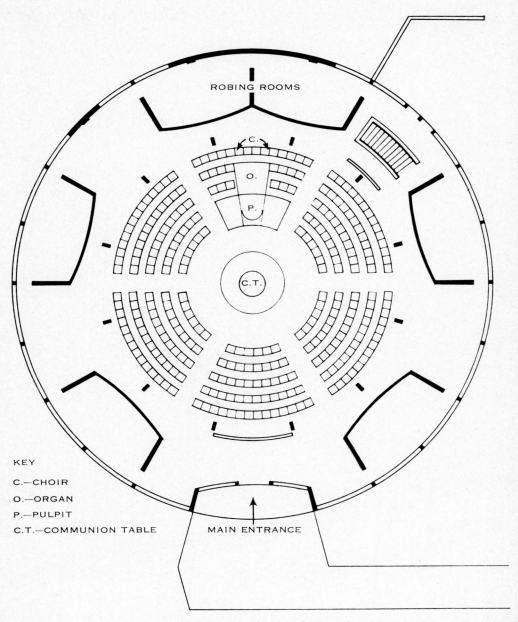

Figure 19. Plan of Bloordale United Church, Toronto, Ont.

Figure 20.   Interior of Bloordale United Church, Toronto, Ont.

BLOORDALE UNITED CHURCH
Toronto
Architect—John Layng, Toronto

This interesting building was completed in 1960 for a newly-formed congregation of The United Church of Canada in a suburb of Metropolitan Toronto. This circular structure illustrates the trend, which we noted in chapter 9, towards an "altar-centred" church so-called (*Figures 19, 20*).

The shell of the building consists of a window wall that completely encircles the auditorium. This wall is non-load-bearing, the tent-like roof being supported by laminated thrusts that rise from the floor to converge at an opening in the top centre of the roof. From this circular opening light floods down upon the communion table, which is located in the exact centre of the nave. The seating of the nave is in concentric circles of pews, one section of which is reserved for the choir. The pulpit and organ are off-centre in the choir section. Vestry and offices are in an outer ring. The building seats four hundred worshippers in its sixty-foot diameter inner circle.

There is said to be a precedent for the round church in early Christian architecture and, more definitely, in the post-reformation period which saw the erection in continental Europe of a number of round churches for Lutheran congregations. In recent years some Roman Catholic congregations on this continent have adopted the circular or octagonal plan, the best known of them being the Shrine of the Little Flower outside Detroit. A gigantic tent-like structure has now been proposed for the Roman Catholic Cathedral in Liverpool, England, and acceptance of this design will likely further popularize the round or altar-centred type of church.

It is interesting to realize that congregations as far apart doctrinally as those mentioned above are able to utilize the central design as suited to their liturgical needs. A suburban congregation of The United Church of Canada feels that the round church admirably expresses the Reformation doctrine of "the priesthood of all believers," whereas a leading Roman Catholic diocese in England asserts that the design expresses "the unity of priest and people in the action of the Mass." It would appear that in architecture, at least, the churches have already attained a significant measure of ecumenicity.

HUMBER VALLEY UNITED CHURCH
Anglesey Boulevard, Islington, Ontario
Architects—Hanks, Irwin and Pearson, Toronto

This building was constructed in two stages. The first unit, the auditorium (angling to the left of the main bulk in the plan [*Figure 21*]), was designed for a congregation that was uncertain of its future growth. As events worked out, the growth proved to be spectacular and the problem confronting the architect was to relate the original scheme to a much larger composition. This was achieved by placing a large mezzanine-type narthex at the juxtaposition of the two masses. Both in the exterior appearance and the interior plan this narthex effectively ties together what would otherwise be a rather confused grouping.

Directly off the main floor of the narthex and in the angle between the auditorium and the nave is the church's administrative and adult centre with offices, vestry, and church parlour forming a compact unit. There is segregation of activities on both floors with what appear to be adequate barriers to sound between the major areas.

The site of the church was happily chosen on an irregularly-shaped lot which shows the whole composition to advantage.

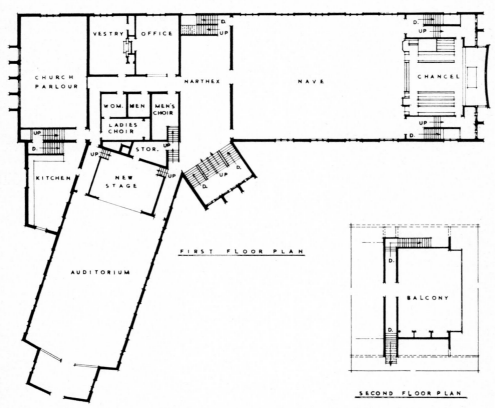

Figure 21. Plan of Humber Valley United Church, Toronto, Ont.

Figure 22.   Yorkminster United Church, Toronto, Ont.

Figure 23.   Interior of Yorkminster United Church, Toronto, Ont.

YORKMINSTER UNITED CHURCH
Toronto
Architect—James A. Murray, Toronto

A church building should do two things. It should serve adequately the needs of the congregation that is going to use it, and it should make an effective witness of its faith to the outside world. The location and appearance of the Yorkminster United Church in Toronto is of interest with regard to this dual function of a church building (*Figures 22, 23*).

This church was constructed in 1956 at the intersection of Yonge Street and Highway 401 in Metro Toronto. This is one of the busiest intersections in the country and an endless stream of traffic flows past this church on both roads. How tempting it would have been to have put an imposing front entrance on this church welcoming all and sundry to its fellowship! A generation ago this temptation would have been irresistible. Conspicuous as this church is, however, there is no way of getting directly to it from the highways and recognition that the church would be attended and supported not by the passers-by but by its own constituency led the architect to locate the main entrance at the south side of the building near the parking lot where the congregation, drawn from the residential areas nearby, actually comes and goes (the modest doorway shown in the photo on the north wall is merely an exit off the nave).

This building is functional also in terms of its witness to the world. This building gives visibility to the faith without trying to impose itself on the passer-by. The very people who speed past this intersection and declaim "It doesn't look like a church!" admit thereby that they know that it is a church and that it has claimed their passing interest. If they are to pursue this interest they must seek a way to get to it. What more can architecture do for the casual passer-by? Only an organic architecture in contemporary idiom can make this kind of witness. A much costlier church could have been built here along traditional lines and the public would not have given it a second look!

CHAPEL, LUNDY'S LANE UNITED CHURCH
Niagara Falls, Ontario
Architects—Parrott, Tambling and Witmer, Toronto

Sound principles of worship should apply to church buildings regardless of their size. The Chapel of Lundy's Lane United Church is actually a small room measuring twenty-three feet by thirty-six feet and yet it contains everything that is needed liturgically for a full diet of public worship and the Chapel is actually used by the congregation for most of its evening services and for other gatherings of a devotional nature where attendances do not exceed its seating capacity of eighty people (*Figure 24*).

Although the ceiling height of this room is merely twelve feet the vertical planking of the east wall, the treatment of the windows which extend to the ceiling and the wide centre aisle give a feeling of spaciousness and height to the chapel that belies its size.

The desk at the left serves for both pulpit and reading desk. The communion table in the centre is free standing. An electronic organ is at the right behind the low mahogany screen. The curvature of the steps leaves space at the right for the baptismal font and for soloist or singers who can stand beside the organ when singing and sit with the congregation throughout the service. The pews of mahogany and white enamel give an early American flavour to the room in keeping with the traditions of a congregation that traces its history back to the late eighteenth century.

Figure 24.   Interior of chapel, Lundy's Lane United Church, Niagara Falls, Ont.

INDEX